The Coalition of Purgatory

Brian T. Seifrit

THE COALITION OF PURGATORY

THE COALITION OF PURGATORY
Published by
Your ESL Story Publishers Ltd.
PO Box 193
Elgin Ontario K0G 1E0 Canada
Publisher@yourstorypublishers.ca
https://yourstorypublishers.ca
Telephone: 613-328-6139
Edition 2
ISBN: 9781928164074
Copyright Brian T. Seifrit © 2004, 2014
All rights reserved.

THE COALITION OF PURGATORY

Dedicated to:

The West Kootenay Coalition for Jumbo Wild and all those who supported their efforts in trying to keep BC wild backcountry, *wild* as it should be. To the Ktunaxa Tribal Council and their people for their undaunted efforts, to all those who feel compassion toward our wild-lands, and who want nothing more than to leave them as they are.

Special acknowledgements obviously go to my wife and kids. To my extended family, and friends for their continued support, and faith in my writing. Thank you all.

Table of Contents

Chapter 1

The bush plane circled Leroy Lake. The droning sound of the plane's engine caught Bryce Ellwood off guard. He wasn't expecting the plane yet, and as he put his camera gear down, he wondered why the plane was showing up now. Walking the short distance to the lake's edge, he waited patiently as the plane approached. He could tell it was Cameron Kane piloting it. Cameron was one of the Kootenay's best bush pilots and he'd been piloting planes since he turned eighteen.

Now in his mid-forties, Cameron had flown hundreds of flights, most into the backcountry. He owned two aircraft, *The Kootenay Green* which was his bush plane, equipped with landing floats, and *The Yellow Mantis,* a helicopter. In twenty-six years, he'd never been late in picking up customers. Nor, was he ever early. Bryce sat down on a big rock, watching the water lap at the rocky shore as the bush plane *The Kootenay Green,* glided across the dark blue water of Leroy Lake, docking next to him.

Cameron stepped out of the plane and onto its landing floats. "Weren't expecting me, were you?"

Bryce reached out his hand, helping Cameron onto the shore. "Nope, wasn't expecting anyone for a couple more weeks. What brings you?"

"I got word from the Conservation Office in New Kootenay that they need you back. They want you to put the work here on hold."

"Really? Why is that?"

"Something to do with another land development in White Swan. I don't know the details, but it was Jackson who told me to come and get you."

"Is that right? You can tell Jackson that you didn't see me. I'm not going back until I'm completely done here. I signed into this project for a six-month term, and Jackson knows it. I plan on seeing it through. You've wasted your time coming here."

"I figured that would be the case, so I brought you

1

more supplies." Opening the door to the plane, he began handing Bryce the few boxes. "I brought everything you wanted me to bring, only a couple of weeks early. I don't imagine I'll be coming back this way for another two, maybe three months. Nevertheless, you can bet Jackson will send someone else. He might even show up here himself to try to convince you otherwise."

"Yeah, well he can come along. I still won't budge. The grizzlies and rest of the animals up here are more important than what Jackson has to say. I have another few months to go before fall, and before I can argue why we shouldn't let that ski resort begin development. Then, and only then will I head back to New Kootenay." Bryce took the last box from Cam and set it down on the shore. "I have coffee brewing, care to stay for a cup?"

"Sure. I have some time left before I'm due back." Each man grabbed a box as they walked the short distance to Bryce's camp. "So, what has your research found?"

"I can tell you that if this land gets developed into a ski resort, the bears and the rest of the game in this area are going to drastically diminish. Might never see a grizzly around here again. They'd be on the trail to extinction, and I can't have that. The animals can't fight this battle alone. They need my protection," Bryce confided to Cam as he handed him a coffee.

"Thank you. The first cup of the day." Cam brought the cup to his nose and inhaled the rich brew's aromatic scent. As the sun crested the Purgatory Mountain range, a mild breeze began to blow, bringing with it the scent of spring. "Man, it sure is nice up here." Cam brought coffee to his lips and took a drink.

"It is, and if I can't convince the powers that be to put a halt on developing this land, the sights you're seeing now won't exist." He took a swig from his own cup of coffee. "Now wouldn't that be a shame?"

"True enough. Why would anyone want to destroy this place with land development? It is a shame. Well, I best get going. I have another flight scheduled." Cam rose from the picnic table under the tent awning. "You have anything you want me to relay to anyone?"

"Nah, but I do have a digital memory card full of photos you can take back to Jackson."

"Sure thing." Cam waited as Bryce retrieved the memory card.

"Got it. Here you go."

The two men walked to the plane and said their good-byes. Bryce watched as the plane scooted across the lake, disappearing in the horizon. Silence again flooded Leroy Lake. Turning on his heels, Bryce tread back to his camp, carrying with him the last two boxes of supplies that Cam had dropped off.

Bryce Ellwood was a freelance writer, researcher and photographer hired by the Canadian Parks and Wilderness Society to do an ecological survey on the Purgatory grizzlies that were in jeopardy of extinction if land development continued in that area. The Society's hope was to put a stop to the hungry land developer Robertar & Robertar who wanted to develop the Purgatory Mountain range into a five-star ski resort.

Bryce was one of the best freelance researchers in British Columbia. At thirty-eight years old, and well versed in environmental issues, he stood just over six-foot tall with sandy brown hair and deep green eyes. Trained in wilderness survival, he was able to live in seclusion. The results of his work always spoke in volumes, and people listened. This campaign was no different. He'd do whatever it took to get the attention of the government, and inform them of the devastation the land development could and would cause if it continued.

When he reached his tent, he began going through the list and checking off the supplies Cam had dropped off. Everything was there. He wasn't sure what he was going to do with a hundred rounds of ammo. *Better safe than sorry I suppose,* he thought as he set the five boxes of ammunition on the table. Noticing a moose crossing the lake, he grabbed his camera, and darted to the shore.

It was a big bull, and it glided across the lake like a small boat, never taking heed of Bryce. He managed to snap six pictures before the big animal finally made it to the other side, disappearing into the dark green forest. *That's moose number four. Got some good images that time,* he smiled. *Now I know why I love this work. There's nothing more gratifying then seeing animals in their own element.*

Today his intent was to hike over to Jack Pine Creek, and with luck, film any bears that might be coming out of hibernation and stopping off for a cool drink. It was early April and the bear population was waking up from hibernation. He had seen only two so far; but all other indigenous game was abundant, including a family of wolverines. The black bear population in the area was estimated at well over sixty, and quite likely into the hundreds. However, the grizzly population according to recent data, showed that only a mere forty-five called the area home. He had seen only two of the forty-five. The others would make themselves present as the months passed, and only time would prove the actual count.

Packing his camera and a lunch, he shouldered his .308 then started off on the three-mile hike over to Jack Pine Creek. It took him the better part of the morning to get there hiking along an old game trail, and by early afternoon he was perched on the banks of the rushing creek. The sound of the crashing water soothed him, and he briefly closed his eyes as the warm afternoon sun beat down on his face. He spent four hours observing the creek that day, but he saw no signs of bear.

He did manage to get pictures of a cougar that appeared from out of nowhere, sitting opposite him on the other side of the creek. It was as though the cougar was posing for him. Finally, the cat ducked into the undergrowth and out of sight. *That's it; go tell all your friends. The more pictures I can get the better off we'll all be.* Sitting back down on the moss-covered ground and reaching into his pack, he retrieved the lunch he carried with him. *Perhaps tomorrow I'll have better luck,* he thought as he finished.

Standing, he turned toward his camp and began the

hike back. At his tent, he unloaded the gear he'd packed and sat down at the table, retrieving a notepad and pen. Then he wrote down the day's events. It was a short entry, but nonetheless an entry. The evening was serene, except for a squirrel chatting in the distance. Bryce put his hands behind his head, listening as the squirrel chorused. It was a relaxing sound, but then nature always was.

Walking to the lakeshore under the glow from the moon he looked out to the lake. To him this was Heaven, this was what nature was all about, beauty and serenity. *Why would anyone want to destroy such a beautiful place,* he wondered, as he skipped a few stones across the lake. Walking along the shore for a couple of minutes, he gathered driftwood for his evening fire. With his arms full, he made his way back to his camp, and with heavy eyes, he poured what was left of his coffee over the fire then and retreated to the tent.

The tent served as both his research centre and his sleeping quarters. It was divided into two sections, sleeping and data-research. Distantly placed behind his tent, was an eight by eight canvas construction that housed a porta-potty with a state of the art enviro-toilet, and a showering area.

Smoothing out his army cot and fluffing up his pillow, he removed his clothes and slipped into his sleeping bag, curious about what tomorrow might bring. He was asleep for only a short while, when he heard the muffled sound of something grunting and snorting. The sound, he knew; came from a bear. Sitting up he reached for his .308, but realised he had left it leaning up against the woodpile outside the tent. Instead, he grabbed the .45 he kept inside and cocked it. He'd once killed a bear with the pistol, although it took four slugs. He'd hated that gun since, wishing he hadn't killed the bear. He knew, though, that at that time, he hadn't had a choice. It was either him or the bear. Now he held the pistol in his hand once more, hoping the bear outside would leave.

After what seemed like eternity, silence again took over. "Thank God," he whispered, pushing the pistol under his pillow. Stepping out into the cool evening, he noticed that the table was knocked over, as was his Coleman camp stove. The boxes of ammunition that were left on the table, were now strewn all over the place, and his clothes hanging on a line outside the tent, were pulled off and stepped on. The empty cardboard boxes that held the supplies were battered and torn. *Thank God,* he thought, *that I stored the food in the cache.*

Bryce picked up the Coleman stove and sat it back on the table. He gathered what he could find of the ammo, but the rest would have to wait until morning. Glancing around and listening, he was satisfied that the bear was no longer in his neck of the woods. Grabbing his rifle, he entered the tent and keeping the .308 within reaching distance, he closed his eyes.

Chapter 2

Bryce woke the next morning to a mist as thick as fog that shrouded his camp and Leroy Lake. It was a cool morning and in the horizon he could make out fresh snow on the peaks of the Purgatory Mountain. It was nothing he wasn't used to. It did however make for a slower start to the day. He was encouraged when he discovered the track of a young grizzly bear. Bending down and looking closer to the imprint left behind, he smiled. *It might be a two-year old,* he thought as he ran his fingers across the edge of the track.

He looked in the direction the bear travelled as it passed by his camp. Finally he rose, walked back to the table and the fresh pot of coffee, and poured a hot steaming cup. Taking the first sips, he set the coffee down and retrieved his camera gear. As he checked the memory cards, lenses and battery packs, he felt as though he was being watched, causing a shiver to run up his spine.

Slowly turning around, he spotted a brown figure, grazing on some patches of mid-spring grass. Raising the camera, he focused in on the figure. A smile crossed his face as he made out a young grizzly. *Well I'll be. You don't seem concerned about me being here, do you, little bear.* By the time he reached for and picked up his digital camera, the bear vanished into the undergrowth and out of sight. Obviously, the bears in the area were coming out of hibernation. He knew the dangers he could now face. Every animal would be ravenous. Now his work would begin. The present dangers were the most important part of his research, filming the forest as it came alive with wildlife and documenting how the animals coped with a new spring.

By 9:00 a.m., the sun finally penetrated the misty morning and he was beginning to feel the chills of the early spring morning leave his body. He inhaled deeply. It was going to be a beautiful day. Today he decided to canoe to the east end of Leroy Lake; the grizzly tracks he found that morning, could wait for a day or two. The research couldn't be based only on the grizzly, although that would indeed be the priority in any case. His research, he knew, must also involve flora and other fauna. The ecological balance depended on all these elements.

He loaded his .35mm camera with film and checked the battery of his digital. Then, tucked both away into their cases, and retrieved his .308 and daypack. Checking the pack over, he made sure it contained everything to sustain oneself for a couple of days if something unexpected happened. Zipping up the tent and shouldering the rifle and pack, he walked to the canoe sitting on the shore a few yards away. It was one of the first twelve-foot canoes he owned, and it had gone with him on many treks. It was short and light, and that's what he liked about it most, not to mention how easily it could be controlled even in mild white-water.

The old fibreglass canoe glided gently into the lake as he paddled his first stroke. Over the years of being roughed up, it was now faded, with a few red, not so faded fibreglass repair jobs, along each side. He smiled as the rhythm of his paddle stroke became fluid, and the trusty canoe obeyed his every thrust. Gliding silently across the water as he neared the rocky north shore, he eased up on his paddle strokes, allowing the canoe to skim slowly on its own. He watched the shoreline-taking note of changes to the flora surrounding the lake.

It was enlightening to see that much growth in such a short time, since he last canoed past that way a few weeks earlier. Back then, snow still covered most of the area, and a thin layer of ice remained along the shore. Now things were coming to life. Removing his digital camera as the canoe drifted, he snapped pictures of the area. Taking up the paddle again, he made a few strokes until his arms needed a rest. Setting the paddle across the bow of the canoe, Bryce inhaled deeply. He loved this feeling of solitude, nothing in life compared to it. For a few moments, he lost himself in the serenity of the here and now. The quiet was broken by the sound of a rumbling avalanche somewhere in the distance. It was the second one he'd heard since arriving at Leroy Lake, but luckily he had not witnessed one first hand.

It was true that the area was plagued with avalanches during the course of a ski season and well into early summer. It was a point brought up countless times, and of course, not many paid heed to. The loss of human life if the resort was developed could be catastrophic. If an unpredicted avalanche woke up from hundreds of years of frozen sleep due to construction, human invasion, waste, or pollution, it would engulf the land holding it back. This would surely be caused by some land developer's activity, and undoubtedly at the cost of a self-sufficient ecosystem. It was a pathetic agenda that the developer was promoting. Nonetheless, it was an agenda that needed to be addressed and opposed. It was Bryce's job to obtain the data and do the research so an opposition could be well-informed.

He squinted as the glare from the early morning sun reflected into his eyes when the east shore came into view. The rocky slopes were still covered with snow, and the shoreline appeared swampy. Finding a place to dock the canoe, he paddled inland a short distance then stepped out onto the rocky shore. Securing the canoe to a stump, he removed his gear, making his way up a slope that led to a marshland; most of which had been runoff and added to the lake's depth at that time of year.

Finding an area dry enough to place his camera and where he was sure he'd get some good photographs of anything ambling along or foraging for food, he sat waiting in contemplation. It seemed like an eternity before the first animal showed itself. It was a white tail deer, a buck at that. "A six point," Bryce whispered as he snapped a few pictures. It wasn't long after that when the animal darted into the forest and out of sight. Smiling he eyeballed the area where the animal once stood. *What a beautiful beast that was.* By late afternoon, he managed to take photographs of a couple more deer, a coyote, and even an eagle circling in the sky, but after a few minutes it tucked its wings and dove out of sight.

Only when he was packing up to leave did he spot the big bear overlooking him up on a ridge. It was close to a quarter mile away, and with his eyes alone, he could tell it was big. Using one of his telephoto lenses, he snapped pictures of the big bear as it coursed its way along the ridge, until it disappeared behind some shrubbery. He kept his camera focused on the shrubs for a few minutes longer, but didn't get another picture. *Not bad for a day of taking pictures*, he reminisced, as he made his way to the canoe. Things changed, though, when he saw that the canoe had became untied, and was sitting near the middle of the lake. Squatting, he looked the situation over and cursed. His only option was to course his way along the rocky shore back to his stationary camp. A hike like that would see him spending the night in the bush. "Damn it all anyway," he muttered as he started the hike back. Leroy Lake wasn't all that big, and one could probably walk the entire circumference of it in one or two days. As long as the old canoe didn't capsize, eventually it would end up on shore.

He walked as far as he could along the shore, until finally making his way up a ravine at the top of a rock bluff. From there, he could faintly make out his camp. Using his binoculars he scanned the area, making sure no animals intruded. Luckily, none had, but he wasn't surprised. Most of the animals kept their distance, as if they were giving him the right to be there.

Descending the rocky cliff and finally making it to the shore, he picked out a sandy area and made up his evening camp. The sound of the lake as it lapped at the shore, drowned out the sounds of silence that night usually brought. A loon echoed in the distance as the pale silvery moon began to shine. Bryce felt at home. He loved the mountains, the animals and solitude, he always had. It wasn't something he was taught. It wasn't something he learned to live with. It was what he loved. Ever since his great Uncle Ben took him on his first snowshoe trek up in the Casino Mountain range when he was eleven, it was his choice to be as he was, and he wouldn't want himself to be any other way. He thanked his Uncle daily for showing him *this* peace.

Others looked upon his life as though he were an introvert. Indeed he probably was. Rarely when he wasn't off working somewhere, or writing an article for the few magazines he wrote for under a pseudonym, did he venture far from his house on the mountain, although it was only a minute's drive to downtown. Nonetheless, for Bryce it was his desire not to do so.

The fire cast shadows along the dark evergreen forest wall only a short distance away. Little billows of smoke puffed up from the fire into the evening air, if they could have made a sound, they would have echoed. Sighing, he walked to the water's edge and skipped a few stones. He could see clear to the middle of the lake with the help from the moon. Faintly he made out his canoe as it bobbed this way and that, looking as though it was drifting inland toward his stationary camp, Bryce smiled, *got a mind of its own that canoe, always did.* He watched as it slowly slipped again into darkness and away from the moonlight.

Preparing for a cold night, he gathered wood for his fire. Sitting near it, he warmed his hands above the flickering flames. Turning to retrieve his pack to get another sweater, he thought he glimpsed the glow of a set of eyes peering out at him from the darkening forest. Averting his eyes in its direction, he shivered, "I hate when that happens," he whispered as he slipped on his overnight sweater.

His .308 was only an arm's reach away, and he knew he could get to it fast if need be. He knew the fire would keep most animals away. Wolverines, though, were known to attack in close proximity of open flames. It was one of the reasons they were more of a threat, and as unique as the bears in that region. Whatever the threat, the flames were his defence. The rifle his last resort. *Keep the fire small and flames high, no animal shall then, pass by.* To this day, he didn't know where he heard that saying. What he did know was that whenever he was out in the bush, he lived by those words. It was a metaphor. Adding a few more sticks to the fire, he nibbled on trail mix. Whatever he saw was long gone. It was completely silent, and a calm came over him like a warm lazy afternoon in July. An hour later, sleepy-eyed, he curled up, and watched the flames dance on the currents of the gently blowing breeze.

Chapter 3

Morning brought with it a frost covered ground, like a light sprinkling of powdered sugar. Bryce stoked the fire, which glowed with embers, warming up his hands and feet as the flames took to life. It had been a cold evening, and so far, a somewhat chilly morn. Standing, he walked the distance to the lake, glancing across it to see if his canoe survived the night. Sure enough, there it was, beached a few hundred yards away from his camp at the end of the lake. He also took note of a set of grizzly bear tracks that led past his lean-to of the night before. They were small compared to the others he saw, and they led right into the lake. He was actually somewhat surprised that one had passed, most likely after the flames from the fire had died down that past night. Bears were quiet swimmers, and if one never heard them enter the water, they'd never hear one swim away. The bear obviously chose to swim around the next point as opposed to going up and over the rocky precipice itself.

Making his way back to the fire, he gathered his camera, letting it warm near the flames. As the sun crested the horizon, he took photographs. The spectacular sunrise slowly made the ground glisten when it made its first appearance of the day, melting the early morning frost and evidence of it, as though it were never there. Dousing the fire, he began the trek back to camp.

By noon, he made his way back, and it had been quite the hike. His shins and knees were scraped from banging them on the rocks as he climbed down the last precipice a few hours earlier. He reminisced now about what he knew of the proposed ski resort. It was hard for him to believe that it would accommodate nearly seven hundred and fifty thousand people a year. It was a sickening thought, yet it could be a reality in a few short years. He tried to picture the proposed hotels and condos, parking lots, stores, and housing, not to mention the ski hills themselves.

His mind drifted to all the animals that needed the seclusion in order to thrive. The proposed ski resort would destroy all that. The animals would be discarded, and mankind's hunger for money and power would be the cause. "People," Bryce whispered, glancing in all directions at the scenery that one-day, might not exist. This was what the world had come to, commercialisation of everything serene, and to some, sacred.

If the valley were left alone it would continue to be a bear haven. It was a place the animals could travel in relative seclusion and free from harm from man. A town with hundreds of thousands of visitors a year and hundreds of permanent residents spelled *disaster* to those who opposed the development. He couldn't even be sure that all his research could or would convince those who were hell bent on developing the land, to change their minds. The good thing was he was given the opportunity to try, and try he would. *Yep, going to give this project the best effort I can, to prevent that travesty from coming to these mountains; only God should be allowed to play God.* His thought was interrupted as he caught a glimpse of movement near the bush line. Looking on, he realised that it was Hector Foxeagle from the Ktunaxa tribe.

Hector moved into the mountain's back in 1988, when the same land developer tried to do the same thing then as they were trying to do now. Back then, Hector swore he'd kill the first person that stuck a spade into the sacred ground of the Ktunaxa. Luckily, it never came to that, as the opposition then was greater than it was now, and the developer was forced to quit his pursued interest. It was hard to believe that sixteen years later the developers had enough fortitude to try again. Bryce and Hector remained friends ever since, although their visits were sporadic over the years, they still conversed whenever time allowed.

Hector was an old Indian guide, living in a cabin near Toby Creek some ten miles from where Bryce was now camped. He was dressed in the same manner as always, with his heavy black and green checker felt jacket and woollen shirt, his brown corduroy pants were tucked into his old leather boots. As always, his long, silver-grey hair was in one braid, going down the centre of his back.

Tied to his belt was a twelve-inch hunting knife and a hatchet, and Bryce knew first-hand how sharp old Hector kept them both. The leather satchel he always carried, dangled off the left side of his waist. His walking stick, without which he never left home, was in his right hand. Hector had carved it out of one piece of birch. The handgrip was carved to fit only his hand. Hidden inside the stick, was a ten-inch honed building spike. The place where the two pieces of his walking stick disjoined was undetectable unless one looked closely, and even then, the hand carved grizzly bears that went around the stick, fooled most.

Hector raised his arm in the air as he approached. "Bryce, it is good to see you up here. The animals have been watching over you. It's what they do for those who look after their interests," Hector said in a heavy Indian accent, as he walked up to the table.

"Hector Foxeagle. Good of you to stop in on me, I thought maybe you'd been run off. Come, sit down I'll pour you a cup of coffee," he poured the old Indian guide a cup and handed it to him. "What do I owe this visit to, Hector?"

"No fee this time," Hector replied with humor. "I have been walking for two days. The animals in this area, they know that the men from down below want again to take away their land. The animals, they're not happy." Hector shook his head. "This time the animals tell me, there might be bloodshed. They say they will protect the white man at Leroy Lake, for he is doing them great favours." Hector took a drink from the cup in his hand.

"I can only do what I can do, Hector. The opposition these men were faced with back in the eighties is far less now than it was then. There is a real possibility that this time they might win."

"I hear the news. I read the papers when they are brought to me. I know how this battle looks from the inside. The Ktunaxa people will not settle for any other decision but the decision to stop this development. There is talk amongst the elders that our brothers and sisters will join us in a stand on these mountains, if those men and their ideas of changing this pristine place do not cease. The battle with the courts and government over our treaty has not been addressed since those men first tried to push their way and their ideas into this sacred mountainous place. We will not settle but for one decision," Hector raised a finger into the air gesturing the number one. "The decision is to stop this madman and his ideals. My people will fight this time, perhaps not with battle-axes, for the pen is mightier than the sword; still we will carry our battle-axes with us into the insurrection.

Today as we sit together, we are friends with all races, creeds, and religions. We speak your tongue, even abide by the white man's law, and follow their acts of perversions. My people have not only died in the years from diseases because of these perversions. We have also been killed because of the white man's laws. They killed us a long time ago when they took our land, and showed us the white man's way. It is much like how my people see these land developers today. All think this land will change too if they continue. And there will be more ideas and laws that your people invent.

It does nothing for the wildlife. If it proceeds then the white man has raped us again. This time though, it will be our land and not our wives, sisters, mothers, and as back then when my people were first introduced to the white man, disease will spread. The disease of nature's demise, I Hector Foxeagle again say the words, I will kill the first white man who sticks a spade into our sacred land. The land of the grizzly, the wolverine, brother moose and deer, the spirit of the eagle, hawk and crow. I, Hector Foxeagle, will be a protector and servant to all animals which travel the same ground as I. I will be a protector of the resources these animals need, including the waters and the fish." Hector sipped again from the coffee in his hand, smiling as he looked at Bryce.

"You certainly have a lot to say, Hector, and I believe every word. However, I won't let you be the protector of all this alone. You and your people have my allegiance. My battle though has to be fought in the House of Commons." There was a short pause as Bryce contemplated. "You know why they call it the House of Commons, Hector?" Bryce asked with a smile. "Cause they couldn't very well call it the House of Common Sense, so they dropped the last four letters and kept the 's'." Bryce began to chuckle. Hector looked at him puzzled for a second then, he too began to laugh.

"Are you sure you are a white man?" Hector asked with cautious humor.

"As far as I know. I've been white all my life, but that doesn't mean I agree with everything my race does. I see things differently than most, and if the choice were mine to make, I think I'd want to be an Indian. Because of your heritage, creed, and all that your people believe in, you'll all likely outlive us white men. It's because of the white man's need for greed and money that areas like this are disappearing at a great rate. Nope, I'd rather be an Indian then a member of a society that caused the demise of our wild-lands and the animals that need them. I'm on your side, Hector, and I plan on doing everything in my power to prevent any further considerations of land development in this area. You have my word." Bryce said, with conviction and intent.

"Indian eh? I will give you an Indian name then, the next time we meet. For now you will still be Bryce, the man at Leroy Lake." Hector rose from the table and took up his walking stick. "Your coffee and conversation has given me the strength to continue with my walk. I will see you again, in June."

"June. That's a month away. Are you sure you don't want to stay and have another cup of coffee?" Bryce asked in hopes the old fellow would agree. It was nice being able to talk to someone, and he still felt the need.

"I said you will see me again in June, but my eyes will see you from time to time, from a distance. I must continue my walk, Bryce. I look forward to sitting with you again, in the summer." Hector turned and walked away. Bryce waved as he tucked into the forest and out of sight.

Standing, he stretched and yawned; it had been an eventful couple of days, and he was beginning to feel weary. He strode into his tent and sat down at the workstation, going through some of his documentation and pictures he'd gathered since arriving at Leroy Lake. The pictures depicted the coming of spring. There were photos of the lake as its ice-covered surface melted, as well as the shrubbery and plant life that began to thrive along the grassy shore, as the ice receded until only a body of deep blue water as smooth as glass, appeared. It took him three weeks to get the sequence of events photographed.

Tossed into the mix were photos of birds, a bear or two, moose and deer, as well as a variety of sunsets and sunrises, it was almost as if one was reliving the change. Putting the photographs back into their respective folders, he read through his notes, adding the past day's events. It was dark when he finished with his last entry. He closed up the notebook and rose from the table. Making his way outside, he inhaled deeply. The pine air was a welcome scent compared to the stale stuffy tent.

Chapter 4

Bryce awoke to yet another cool and misty morning. Soon enough the cold mornings would end, and by May, the weather would finally change and warm up. Until then, he'd have to live with the hazy chilled mornings, but they were refreshing if nothing else. Usually by 10:00 a.m., the sun was out full bore. Today however, the sky was clouded over and it looked like rain.

Looks like I stick around here today. Don't want to be stuck out there somewhere once that rain comes. That's all right though. I have work I can get caught up on, he thought. The young grizzly he'd seen a few days earlier was again in his view some distance away along the bush line. He watched as the young bear grazed on sprouts of mountain grass. He walked to the back of his tent then and squatted there, where. he had a clear view of the bear.

Indeed, it was a young one, and he wondered if its mother was nearby. Usually that would be the case for such a young animal, but scanning the area he saw no other bear. That didn't necessarily mean that the bear's mother wasn't near, just that he couldn't see her. He watched the young bear for a few more minutes, until finally the young cub stood on its hind legs and looked directly at him. The two made eye contact; briefly staring at one another. The young bear dropped back to all fours and dashed into the undergrowth, crashing through the forest as though it saw a ghost. Bryce smiled, shaking his head at the bear's lack of gracefulness. *Cubs are always clumsy at that age.*

Turning on his heel he went back to the table and poured a coffee. *I sure hope that momma bear is around, a young cub like that with no mother hasn't got much of a chance in this wilderness.* Standing from the table, he gathered his rifle and camera, walking the distance to where he'd seen the cub. He followed the tracks, maybe walked a quarter of a mile when he heard the familiar, almost human, cries of a bear. Tilting his head, he tried to pinpoint the direction the cries were coming from. Finally, he spotted the cub, ducked behind some shrubbery, and using his camera, he focused in on the area.

The cub lay next to his mother. Bryce was hoping to see the animal rise or breathe, and he waited patiently, but after a long silence he realised she was dead. He stood with caution, walking within a few yards of the two bears. The cub instinctively rose, darting behind a mountain ash. Approaching the big female, he could tell that she'd been dead for a few days, and it was a miracle that the cub survived as long as it had. Kneeling beside the carcass, he put his hand on the animal as if he were petting it. There were no visible wounds that he could see, other than the marks left by another animal that fed on the carcass, perhaps even the cub itself. Nothing told him how or why she'd died.

A feeling of uselessness overwhelmed him as he took photos. All he could do was hope and pray that the young cub would survive. He realised then, that what he needed to do was help the cub as much as possible. There was no way he could turn his back on the orphaned cub. It was faced with starvation and would be a cruel and painful way for the cub to die. Standing, he looked toward the big mountain ash the young cub was hiding behind. Slowly he approached it, whispering gently. He could see the young cub looking at him. "It's all right, little fellow. I won't hurt you." He put his hand out, gesturing to the cub. "Come here, it's okay. You're going to need some help and I'll do whatever I can to help you. These mountains will be unrelenting to a little fellow like you. Come on, it's all right." The cub approached and sniffed at his hand, its wet nose touching the back of it.

"See I don't want to hurt you." The cub backed away again and lay down. "You know where I'm at. I'll put some food out for you. In the meantime," he reached into his pocket and pulled out a big piece of jerky, "here is some jerky for you." He tossed the meat near the cub then rose and started for his camp, glancing back one last time. He was pleased to see the young cub sniffing the meat and finally eating it.

Back at camp he went directly to the food cache, grabbed a few cans of salmon, and canned corn, retrieving one of his bigger cast iron pots, he opened the contents of the cans and dumped them in. *That ought to get his attention,* he thought as he walked to the bush line and set the pot down on a log. By the time he'd drank a second cup of coffee, the cub was nearing the pot. It sniffed at the air and approached with caution.

He watched as the bear cub knocked the pot over and began routing through the food left for him. It looked in Bryce's direction then continued feeding. It took a few days for the cub to come close, but by April 24, when he woke that morning, he was relieved to see that the cub found a place to curl up, even if it was on his favourite sweater, which he absently had left on the table the night before. A smile crossed his face as he silently sat down and looked on at the sleeping cub. Swivelling in his seat, he startled the young cub, which stood up, and darted to the undergrowth. It never went far.

"It's all right. I didn't mean to frighten you. Come on back, I have some food for you." He stood up, tossing the cub a piece of smoked sausage. "You go ahead and eat that. I'll get you some salmon in a minute, and if you like, I can mix you up some powdered milk. Come on, it's okay." Walking closer, he held out his hand. The cub briefly shied away then approached, this time licking the back of his hand. Its tongue felt rough like that of a cat's. "See little guy, I'm your friend, come on follow me back and I'll get that salmon and milk for you." The cub backed away.

"All right, have it your way. I'll get the food for you and put it in your pot; you can come and get it whenever you like." Walking to his food cache, he grabbed two cans of salmon and the milk powder, noting that he was running low on both. He mixed the milk with the water from the salmon and added some vegetable oil that he used to fry potatoes. It looked like thick soup, and smelled awful. He added a little more water until he thought it might be close to the consistency of the mother's milk. Tossing another sausage into the mix, he set it down near the back of the tent.

A few minutes later the cub reluctantly crept up to the pot and began feasting. He photographed the cub as it licked the pot clean then it slowly backed away and hid behind the tent. Bryce waited a short while before he walked around behind the tent, finding the cub lying down and sleeping. Quietly he retrieved the sweater the cub slept on earlier and he set it beside him. "There you go, this can be yours," he whispered as he reached out, and stroked the fur on the cub's back. The cub didn't twitch or open an eye. Standing, he walked back to the table. *Well Bryce Ellwood, looks like you've just taken on the role of provider for that little beast. Likely, he's going to eat you out of house and home.* He smiled at the sentiment. *Guess I best radio in for some more supplies, got two mouths to feed now.*

He watched as the first raindrops began to fall for the second time in as many days. Sitting at the table sheltered by the awning of his tent, he watched the rain pelt the lake like millions of bugs scooting across it. He was surprised when the cub peeked around the corner as if waiting to be invited under the shelter. "Getting a little bit wet are you? Well come on under here, don't be afraid."

The cub looked at him for a few seconds then ambled under the awning next to the woodpile. "I'll get you your sweater. Hang tough." He stood and ran around back of tent, grabbing the sweater, which by now was sopping wet. "It's a little damp, but will dry in no time. That's why I liked it so much. Here, it's yours now." He laid the sweater down next to the cub. "Go ahead, lie down on it." The cub sniffed at the gift then curled up and closed its eyes.

"It is hard to believe that in no time at all you'll be hulking over it, but for now little friend, enjoy it." Looking out across the lake, his mind drifted in and out on what he might have got himself into. All that mattered though was that the cub needed his help. That was why he was there, to help, and help he would at any cost. It was true he might be faced with adversity, because he'd taken the cub under his wing, but adversity never prevented him from doing what he believed to be good, and it wasn't about to start now. Not now, not ever, he was in it for the long run whatever the consequences may be. Life was too short to constantly worry about adversity.

That is how he thought, and that was how he lived. Adversity was nothing more to him than a nine-letter word, like *horseshoe*. By mid-afternoon the rain subsided, and the sun peeked out from behind the rolling black clouds. The day was going to turn out nice after all.

Rising from the table, he walked to the lake. The bear cub lolled behind, still curled up on his old sweater. The air was filled with the freshness that only comes after a good downpour. He inhaled deeply. He always loved that bouquet of newness. Looking out across the lake, he skipped a few stones, contemplating what to do for the rest of the day. There was some work he needed to catch up on, but he felt lazy. The work could wait.

Walking along the shore, he retrieved his canoe. Taking it by one of the ropes attached to the bow, he pulled it along, walking in ankle-deep water. The canoe skimmed across the surface like a dragonfly, barely making a ripple. Docking it in its usual spot, he walked back to his camp. Spotting the cub, he realised that it had taken an interest in a porcupine that now scooted toward safety, as the bear cub nipped at its backside. Curiosity finally got the better of the bear as it got too close.

The porcupine stopped and raised its haunches, whacking the cub with its tail. The cub squawked in pain and fell over backwards. It brought its front paws up to its snout, now full of quills, swatting at it as if hoping to remove the painful daggers sticking out. Crying, the cub ran in circles as the pain from the quill's shot to every muscle of its face, ears, and eyes. Finally dizzy, the cub sat down, wobbling for a minute before it fell over. Bryce was both laughing at the hilarity of it all, at the same time concerned about how much pain the bear cub was in.

"A lesson learned is a lesson gained," he said to himself as he approached the whining cub, removing his Weatherman knife, he snipped the end off each quill and used the pliers to pull the quills out. It was no easy task holding the cub and avoiding its teeth and claws as they dug into his lap. He was bitten a few times, but it was nothing serious, as the little cub didn't have much of a bite yet. By the time he was pulling out the last few quills, the cub finally relaxed.

"There that's it. If you only behaved like that in the beginning, we'd have been done a long time ago. I guess you won't be playing with porcupines again. They pack quite a punch, don't they? There are a lot of other things you best learn to stay away from, for example, if you ever see an animal with a white strip down its back, don't expect it to play nicely." Chuckling he let the bear cub go. It darted this way and that then finally to the shore, where it splashed around and lapped up a drink or two.

Bryce stood and walked the shore with the cub splashing and dashing in front of him. *I still haven't come up with a name for that little fellow. What about Leroy? Nah, Brutus, maybe, no sounds mean. I know, how about Prophet? That sounds all right. Then again maybe not. A name will come to me soon enough, I'm sure.* Bryce brainstormed for a second longer. "I got it, Redeemer. That's it. It means prophet in a sense. How do you like that little fellow?" he asked the cub as if it would reply. "From now on that's what I'll be calling you. When you hear Redeemer, it means you. That's how I'll call you for dinner too, you best memorise how it sounds, all right, Redeemer?" The bear cub stopped for a moment and looked back then picked up his pace again as he continued frolicking in the water. *I guess he gets it.* Bryce smiled.

The sound of a helicopter in the distance made him and the cub stop short of camp, as they listened. Redeemer tilted his head and as the sound became louder, he ran for cover to some undergrowth. Bryce looked in the direction the sound was coming from. At the end of the lake and in the horizon, the craft appeared, flying in his direction. As it got closer, he could tell it was a forestry helicopter. The helicopter circled once then landed in the clearing behind his tent, causing the tent to flap ferociously until the rotor blades stopped spinning.

The passenger door opened and out stepped Conrad Jackson. Bryce shook his head. *I can't believe he'd actually come up here. He isn't getting me to leave here, no matter what his problem is.* Waving to Jackson, he approached. "Hey, Jackson. What brings you way up here?"

"As if you don't know." Conrad Jackson reached out his hand and shook Bryce's. "How has it been going up here?"

"About as good as it can go. I'm glad that you showed up. I need to order more supplies to be delivered in the next couple of weeks. I was going to call you on my cell, but figured I could wait a day. Tell me Jackson what brings you?"

"Seems we have a problem up near White Swan. Some hikers found one of our tagged moose as well as a young grizzly in that area, they appeared to have been butchered. I guess you could say we're faced with a bit of a poaching problem up there, on top of everything else. It is more complex than that, though."

"Really, doesn't sound complex to me. Send a couple Conservation Officers up there to figure it out or the RC's. I'm not interested in an issue like that, give me a break. I mean really what am I supposed to do, snap photos? I'm not the law or even a conservation officer. I'm a freelancer, Jackson, who was hired to do a six month study up here on the effects of any further land developing."

"The big picture is that the developer who wants to do work up here, is the same one who is doing excavating in White Swan. I assumed you could take a few of your brilliant pictures. You get them on film doing something fallacious, it would certainly add to your collection of data. Maybe put these guys right out of business before they even get a chance to start wrecking the Purgatorys."

"Jackson, my work is here." Bryce sighed; he wanted to help, but the work he was committed to now was more important. "I'll give you the name of an associate of mine who also does exceptional work. That's all I can offer. That is of course if you're interested?" he responded as he contemplated the situation in White Swan. His mind was made up though; he was staying right where he was.

"If that's your final answer, I don't imagine I could sway you. What's the name of your associate then?"

"Cameron Kane's kid brother, Dillon. You can reach

him at Cam's house. Let them know I sent you."

"We we're going to ask him first but Cam said he was off somewhere and wasn't due back until late June. I can't remember where it was that he left for."

"Really? That sucks, what about one of your guy's from your office?"

"Yeah it'll have to be." Jackson replied with defeat. "Got that list of stuff you want sent back?"

"Same as always Jackson, except of course ammunition, I got over a hundred rounds already. If I think of anything more I'll call ahead a few days before the supplies are scheduled."

"All right. I'll get the stuff ordered and sent your way in two weeks. That'd put us where? May 14, or there about. I'll get the stuff to you then." Jackson said as the two men turned and walked the short distance to the waiting helicopter. Bryce shook Jackson's hand, wished him luck in solving the White Swan dilemma. The helicopter rotor started to rumble and whistle, as Jackson opened the door and stepped inside.

Bryce ducked his head and darted away from the now whipping rotor blades. Stopping short of his tent, he turned and waved again to Jackson, who was giving him the finger. Bryce chuckle, "right back at you!" he hollered, returning the gesture.

Finally, the silence of the mountains returned. Looking in the direction he last saw Redeemer. The cub was nowhere in sight. He waited patiently in hopes that he would show himself. After almost thirty minutes and still no sign of the cub, he called out for him then put out some food. Eventually it would respond to the smell.

On occasion, he hollered out Redeemer's name, but to no prevail. A rustling coming from inside his tent caught his attention. Startled at first, he cautiously approached it. Using a long pole that he picked up, he guardedly pulled back the tent door open. "Whoa, little house wrecker, I'd say. There you are, I've been calling you for the past twenty-minutes. I guess you decided here was safer than out there, huh. Well, welcome inside." Laughing he approached the cub, which by now was no longer afraid of his presence. "There is some food for you out back. You best get to it, before that old porcupine decides he wants it. Then you'll have to fight him for it."

The sun set early that day and by 8:00 p.m., Bryce retreated inside. By eight thirty he was sound asleep.

Chapter 5

The morning was crisp when Bryce and the cub headed outside. The sun was already reflecting off the lake, and a mild breeze gently blew. "It is going to get hot, Redeemer. This is the warmest morn since I've been here. There isn't even any frost today. Maybe spring has finally sprung." Walking over to the thermometer that hung on one of the awning poles, he saw that it read a warm 10 degrees C. It was a normal temperature for that time of day and year, up about 2 degrees from the morning prior.

"Yep, the warmest morning so far." Taking a few steps back, he sat down at the table. "Today is Sunday. I don't do anything on Sundays. Tomorrow, though, we have to get something done. Likely, we'll head over to Jack Pine Creek. I'm sure things have changed since I was last there. Anyway, today we'll take a walk along the lake and check out the foliage and stuff, but nothing overexerting."

Igniting his camp stove he prepared breakfast for Redeemer. He didn't have to invite the cub to take the meal a second time. Redeemer dug in with his front paws and when he was finished he needed a bath. It looked as though he'd rolled in the slop. Finally, finding his way over to the sweater he curled up, yawned, and was soon out like a light.

An hour and half later, at 10:00 a.m., while Bryce was sitting at the table writing in a note pad, Redeemer came up behind him and put his paws on the table. "Did you have a good cub nap? You've been out for almost two hours. Are you rested enough to take a walk?" Bryce closed the note pad he'd been writing in. The cub went back on all fours and started to walk away. "I guess that's a yes."

He grabbed his camera and daypack, which he kept stocked with power bars, waterproof matches, first-aid-kit, and such, for those 'what if' situations that sometimes happened. They walked south along the lakeshore. Redeemer frolicked and ran ahead, stopping now and again to take in the scents of Leroy Lake. Bryce snapped pictures of the bear cub as well as the new foliage that was starting to grow. It was tranquil and intoxicating, especially with the added company of the cub.

Here in the middle of nowhere, on top of the world, he was walking as one with the grizzly. *What a turn of events,* Bryce reminisced, *from being one-man to being one-man with a grizzly cub. He's going to grow like a weed in the coming months, by the time he's full-grown he'll likely weigh eight hundred pounds, in all likelihood more. He won't be eating canned salmon and leftovers then, he'll be eating the whole salmon, and I'll be eating the leftovers, cause he'll be too big for me to argue with.* He chuckled. *Yep I'm in for it, undoubtedly and indeed.*

Deciding to rest for a few minutes, he sat down on an old log, pulled out a couple of power bars from his knapsack and tossed one to the cub. "That one is fruit and nut. I'll eat the chocolate one." Redeemer sniffed it then snaffled it up. "That's pretty good eh? They're good for you too. Well, good for me anyway, but I guess some fruit and nut's isn't going to hurt you. It's the kind of stuff bears are supposed to like and I can tell you liked that. Let's see if I have another fruit and nut in here."

Reaching into his pack, he pulled out the four remaining power bars. "This one is fruit and nut, got another too," he held them up. "The others are chocolate raisin and peanut butter crème, which is another one you'd probably like. I'll let you have that one later." Removing the foil wrapping from the second fruit and nut bar, he held it out. The bear cub approached and took it from his hand. "That a boy. You took that nice." He patted Redeemer, who was at his feet chewing the last of the second power bar.

A rustling in some nearby undergrowth caught his attention. Slowly rising he looked on. The cub picked up the scent of whatever it was and he sniffed the air. In an instant a cougar bounded out of the undergrowth and darted up the slope behind them. Jumping back, he armed himself with the daypack, if nothing else he could use it to swing at the cougar and with luck scare it off. To his relief the cougar continued ascending the slope and finally was out of sight.

His heart was beating a mile a minute. The cub was on

his hind legs trying to be as ferocious as possible, but he looked no more frightening than an over stuffed teddy bear. "By God, you scared him away," Bryce said in humor as he cautiously looked around. "That cat is long gone by now, good job in scaring him off buddy, good job indeed." He nodded as he pat him, his eyes still affixed on the slope. "What do you say we finish this walk on another day. With that polecat out and about, we're probably better off near camp. If we let him do his thing, he'll leave us alone. We probably interrupted his rabbit hunt. Come on Redeemer let's head back."

By 2:00 p.m., the pair was sitting under the tent's awning back at camp, shaded from the hot afternoon sun. "Today wasn't a total waste. Got some good images of you, and some of the new foliage that's started to grow." Turning, he looked to Redeemer who was again snoozing. Smiling he turned back and looked out over the lake, his hands behind his head and legs stretched out under the table. *Another lazy Sunday,* he thought.

Beginning to doze, he was startled by a female voice. "Hello there."

He quickly sat up and looked in the direction of the voice. There in front of him was a young woman sitting atop a big brown horse. She had long sleek black hair and eyes as blue as Leroy Lake. She wore a buckskin jacket with tassels, and blue jeans with brown leather chaps. On her feet, she wore knee high moccasins. She was a sight of sheer beauty, and his eyes almost popped out of his head. He hadn't seen a woman so pleasing in a long-time. He blinked his eyes a couple of times to satisfy himself that it wasn't a dream and that indeed there was a woman on a horse in front of him. "Hello, back." he said as he stood. "Is there something I can help you with?"

"Maybe," the woman replied, as she looked him over. "So, you're Bryce?"

"Yes, yes I am. And you are?" he asked with curiosity.

"I'm Rayne-Bow Foxeagle, but I go by Rayne, that's 'Y, N, E.'; my grandfather is Hector," the woman replied as she dismounted her horse, walking up to him with her hand extended. Bryce reached out his and the two shook. The woman's name and voice echoed in his head like poetry.

"Nice to meet you, Rayne. Is there something wrong with old Hector?" he asked with sincerity and concern, all the while astonished at her presence and beauty.

"I'm not sure. I haven't seen him. He was expecting me, but when I arrived on Thursday, he wasn't around. He left me a note saying he was going on a walk. Said he was stopping by the researcher's camp at the head of Leroy Lake, which I assumed and have confirmed to be you. Has he been to see you?"

"Yes, as a matter of fact he was here last week on the 21st, I think it was Wednesday. I can't believe he hasn't made it back to his cabin, yet. You don't suppose something happened to him, do you?"

"It's hard to say. Sometimes he takes long walks. A week isn't unusual or out of character. If he doesn't return in a few more days, I'll be more concerned. If you saw him last Wednesday and he seemed healthy then there is no need to worry yet. Did he seem his usual self?" Rayne asked.

"I think so. Yeah, I'd say he was his usual self. He claimed he'd been walking for two days already. He was showing no ill-effects from it, he was as chipper as always," Bryce responded as he shrugged his shoulders.

"Good then we shouldn't worry yet." She looked out across the lake and smiled. "You have a beautiful view of the lake from here."

"Yes, it sure is. Hey, if we aren't going to worry about Hector for a day or two and if you're in no hurry to get back, can you stay and join me for a coffee? I'd certainly appreciate the company," he hesitantly asked with hope.

"Thank you. Sure, I'll join you for a coffee." Smiling she sat down at the table. "I see you have a friend." She pointed at the bear cub.

"Ah, yeah. He was orphaned a while back, but I didn't find him until a few days ago. I couldn't see myself letting him die. I know it probably wasn't one of my better decisions, but I guess I have a soft spot for misfortunes like that. I think he might be a yearling."

"Grandfather would know," she replied, as he handed her a cup of steaming hot coffee. "Thank you. Tell me what do you feed a bear cub?"

"I feed him whatever he'll eat, so far I haven't found anything he won't." He chuckled. "Mostly I feed him stuff high in fat and protein. He hasn't got sick, so I guess what I've been feeding him agrees with his stomach." There was a short period of silence as the two newly acquainted friends sat in self-contemplation, waiting for the other to speak. "Umm say, would you like to take a walk down near the lake?" he finally spit out.

Rayne looked at him and she smiled. "You wouldn't happen to be coming onto me, would you?" she coyly asked.

"Maybe a little," he humorously admitted. "I haven't been in the presence of a beautiful woman like you in quite some time. I freely admit that your beauty takes me back. It would be a shame if I offered you only a coffee, and not a walk down near such a peaceful body of water." He gestured toward the lake.

Rayne's face was glowing with her smile; she hadn't been spoken to like that in a long-time. "For your honesty, it'll be my pleasure to walk with you." Rayne replied as she stood up.

"No. It'll be my pleasure to walk with, and be in the presence of an enchantress, as beautiful as you, Rayne-Bow Foxeagle," Bryce responded with a smile all his own. The two walked side by side, the short distance to the lakeshore. Redeemer followed close by; he too seemed to be taken back by Rayne. "Do you visit with Hector often?" Bryce asked out of curiosity and to converse with the lady to his right.

"Yes. I visit with grandfather as regularly as I can. Usually from May to September; then I return to the university. I'm studying anthropology, biology, and a few other *ologies* as well. It's environmental sciences that interest me most, you know, ecology and such, but I'm also partial to social science. Anthropology is a real blast."

"Yeah. Really, I like all those things too. What university are you attending?"

31

"U of A. Another four years to go and I'll have my BA in science and arts and a degree in Anthropology. I can't wait. I'll be free. Free at last from all the hustle and bustle of the big city and big shots. I have plans on residing on grandfather's land over in Toby Creek for a few years and write a book, or just get to know myself again. I'm tired of living in my one room apartment, and not having a forest or mountain to look at for miles. Eating the same Chinese food every Monday, Wednesday, and Friday then eating at fast food restaurants in between," Rayne went on.

"I hear you. I went through all that too. Only thing was I couldn't stand it, and gave up perhaps a little soon. I would have had all my BA's and degrees as well, but the mountains kept calling me. Plus I got a decent break and was given the opportunity to do whatever it is I do now." Shrugging his shoulders, he snickered as he reminisced. "Yep, I live in the mountains as much as possible. I take every opportunity and dirty job I can get that involves doing so. There is nothing more gratifying."

"I guess your research up here is in regard to the proposed Purgatory Resort?" Rayne asked already knowing the answer.

"That's what they tell me. Six months of bug bites, cuts, bruises, and no amenities whatsoever. I wouldn't have it any other way."

"Man, I wish I had your job."

"If I could give it to you, I still wouldn't."

"I wouldn't give it a way either," responded Rayne, as the two finally made it to the lakeshore. The lake was calm, not a ripple lapped at the shore. Behind them and to the west was a spectacular sunset, reflecting in the sedate waters in full colour. Even the trees mirrored as though one was looking at them through a pain of glass. Turning, they gazed at the colourful horizon.

"Wow, that is a pretty sunset. I haven't seen one like that in years. I miss stuff like this all the time, being cooped up in classes all day and then my apartment at night, while I cram from the next day's big exam, pop quiz, discussion or whatever else is due," Rayne commented. How she wished the four years had already passed.

"Well if in four years all this is the same and you stand right where you are now at this same time of day and month, you'll likely see another sunset even better than this one. No two sunsets are alike. Each expresses a turn of events, life, death, happiness, and sorrow. All those colours represent the coming of day's end and the beginning of a tomorrow that never comes. Indeed you are right, it is beautiful." He was sounding philosophical and he knew it, but that's how he looked upon sunsets; he always had.

"That was poetically philosophical. I loved it. Everybody should look at a sunset like that. I know I will from now on." Rayne commented as she looked at Bryce, watching him gaze at the coming of day's end.

"Take it with you to the free world, Grasshopper," he said in his best David Caradine voice. "It is wisdom you must propagate amongst your Canadian peers." He looked at Rayne to see her looking back at him. She had a smile on her face, and as their eyes met they both broke out into a giddy laughter.

Time slipped by as it always did, and before the sun had completely set, the two friends bid each other goodbye and Rayne headed back to Toby Creek, promising she'd stop back mid-week. He watched and waved as she and her horse entered the undergrowth, fading from his sight. Inhaling deeply, he sighed. *What a beautiful woman. Why didn't Hector ever tell me his granddaughter was so beautiful. I'll be having words with him.* Chuckling to himself, he walked back to his tent.

"For a lazy Sunday, the day couldn't have turned out better. Never would I have expected such a sight of beauty to end up at my front door. What do you say, Redeemer?" he questioned the cub as it sat on its behind staring at him. "We have something to look forward to come mid-week, another visit from Rayne-Bow Foxeagle. That name conveys more than a name." Bryce looked to Redeemer, who was almost begging for some food.

"I get it. You're not interested in friendly chit-chat. You'd rather be eating. All right, I suppose it is that time again. I'll get something fixed up for you." He continued to reminisce about the enchantress he met that day. He guessed her age to be in the late twenties, early thirties. Nonetheless, she was one hundred percent woman. A mantrap is what she was. Intelligent, witty, sensual, she was everything sunrises and sunset weren't; she was a *Rayne-Bow* of colour. Scooping some things into Redeemer's pot, he topped it off with some oatmeal.

"Here you go." He set the pot down. "This ought to keep you full until tomorrow. It has everything you like. We'll mix up some pancakes in the morning, and make extra's for snacks later in the day. Got some egg powder left as well, it probably wouldn't hurt to scramble some," he mentioned as he walked back to the table. Before he was even settled, Redeemer had engulfed the concoction set out for him, and was licking his chops.

"You can't be serious. I just set that out. For a little fellow you have an enormous appetite. There must be something missing in your diet. How would a momma bear keep up with a ferocious appetite like yours? I guess I better find something more appropriate and filling then what I've been feeding you." Pausing for a minute, he thought of what else he could be feeding the cub, if indeed, he was missing something in his diet, but nothing came to mind. He was feeding the cub vegetables, meat, grain, nuts, all the things a bear might find in the wild. Granted only the nuts and vegetables were in their raw form. The meat and everything else had always been smoked, cooked, or canned. He scratched at his chin. "Then again, it could be you just like to eat, huh."

Redeemer by now settled on the sweater and was yawning, sleepily looking on. "Yeah. I suppose it is time to call it a night. We got a few miles hike ahead of us tomorrow. It is best that we get rested." Standing from the table he stretched, looking around at the darkening wood. Night had come to Leroy Lake and another lazy Sunday ended.

Unzipping the flap to his tent, he invited Redeemer in, but the bear neglected the offer and instead curled up tighter and closed his eyes. "I'll leave the bottom open a bit so later when the coyotes howl, you got a way in." Stepping into the tent, he closed the flap part way. The army cot was as welcoming as any bed. Kicking off his boots he pulled off his socks and slipped out of his Levi's, tossing his shirt at the foot of his bed. He fluffed up his pillow then crawled beneath the cool sheets.

Chapter 6

Bryce and Redeemer made their way to Jack Pine Creek before 11:00 a.m., that Monday morning. Things indeed had changed since his last visit. The foliage and creek had both grown. The runoff from the mountains added to the creek's size and force, as it swept by them like rolling thunder. *Wow, she has sure grown. It wasn't nearly as fast and ferocious, as it is now, when I was here last. The runoff from the mountains must be full bore,* he thought, as he and Redeemer sat on the grassy shore.

"I don't think there's going to be many animals taking a cool drink at this spot. It's too fast here; maybe we should hike up the creek a bit. There has to be a drinking pool along it somewhere. What do you say? Come on, we'll go upstream." Rising, the two began hiking along the creek staying on the high side of the shore.

Making their way up and over a couple of rocky outcrops, they approached a large pool of water. It was exactly what he'd hoped to find. *Now this is where we'll get some good photos. A lot of game will likely be using this spot to quench their thirst.* He found an area that was somewhat level and covered in moss, obscurely hidden behind some bigger rocks and a few bushes. It would be the perfect spot to set up the camera on auto. It was early enough, he guessed, that they could hike up the creek another couple of miles. Then, later that afternoon, head back and gather the camera, and with luck, get some surprising results.

It took a couple of minutes to set up the camera so that the focus was set on the panoramic view covering the entire body of water from shore to shore. As he set the camera, Redeemer took it upon himself to be the first on film. He strutted over to the refreshing pool and frolicked, which helped with the set up. Satisfied, Bryce sat down on the moss-covered ground shaded by the over-hanging branches of a big cedar. He let Redeemer frolic for an extra few minutes while he rested, contemplating the serenity. Finally rising and dusting himself off, he called for the cub. "Redeemer, come on little fellow, we're all set here. Let's hike on a bit," he called as he gathered his daypack and .308. The bear cub came to his calling, sopping wet and stinking to high heaven. "Whew, you bears sure stink when you're wet. Come on, this way." Redeemer clipped alongside him, often fighting with the low shrubbery, which Bryce could easily step over. The thicker the bush the slower young Redeemer traipsed on.

Finally breaking through the thick forest that skirted the creek, the two companions came to an area that opened up, thanks to the logging efforts of some beavers. There were four dens, and a huge dam, that either broke or was in the process of being built, as it wasn't yet to the other side. There was definitely a pooling effect going on though. The beavers picked the location because of two things; the creek slowed at that point and lazily rolled by. The second reason was the amount of foliage that grew on the far south-facing slope, which gradually sloped into the creek.

"What do you think of that? A family of beavers, maybe even a couple of families seemed to have moved in or had been living here for a few years. That's all right, though; it's a great place for beavers." Pausing he looked toward one of the beaver dens then back to the south slope. "The south slope is full of vegetation, plus the creek doesn't scream by. It just rolls on like a lullaby," he said in a smooth rhythmic voice, as though he were a poet.

"I say we stop here. We'll eat lunch and maybe I'll get lucky enough to snap some pictures of the beavers with the digital. We'll get a few of the dens and area as well. It would be cool though to get a couple of the beavers themselves." He removed his pack, rifle, and camera case. Sitting down he thumbed through his pack pulling out some jerky and a couple of power-bars and unsalted peanuts. "This is lunch, Redeemer. Here is a piece of jerky for you to start with." He handed the bear cub the jerked meat and Redeemer took it as gently as always.

Biting into his piece of jerky, he removed his digital camera and focused in on the beaver dens. He took ten frames of the wood and mud huts that the beaver engineers built. It was amazing that the beaver built their huts as they did, like little engineers matching every stick or glob of mud to make the best fit, using their teeth as saws, their paws as hammers and flat tails as trowels.

It always amazed Bryce, how much ingenuity and skill the beaver had. By the time he put the camera down, Redeemer had helped himself to the bag of peanuts, using his front paws to root through Bryce's pack, destroying three rolls of unused film.

"Hey, hey come on get out of there." Bryce commanded, waving his hand at the cub. Redeemer shied away then rose on his hind legs, showing some attitude. "Never mind. That is not Redeemer's pack, there is stuff in there that could be wrecked or broken," he responded firmly.

Redeemer went back onto all fours and apologetically rubbed up against him. "Ah, that's all right. That film wasn't even opened yet, no big deal. Keep in mind though, that if my digital camera was in there, you could have really done some damage to it, I don't imagine it's bear proof." Removing the foil wrapper from one of the power bars, he handed it to Redeemer.

"We'll sit for a while longer and then head back. If you want to take a swim, this is as good of place as any," he commented. Instead of going for a swim however, Redeemer stayed back with him, lolling in the shade, listening to the same captivating silence. Taking notice of a brown figure on the south slope near the top, he used his digital camera to try and focus in on the figure as it slowly cut across the top, travelling easterly. Because of the distance, he didn't take a picture, nor was he able to determine the kind of animal it was before it disappeared over the top. He shrugged with acceptance.

"Well, it doesn't look like the beavers are going to show. We best get a move on and head back down the creek. Maybe the other camera snapped a few good frames of something. Come on, little bear." Throwing the pack over his shoulders and grabbing the rifle, the two set off downstream, with Bryce deciding that the next time he came to the creek, he'd camp out for a couple of days up at, or near the dams. That way he could take the time to hike up the south slope and check the type of vegetation that grew there. That would be next time though.

The hike downstream took less time, and within an hour they were standing next to his camera. The tripod hadn't fallen over and eight new frames were added to the picture count. "Had some action down here it looks like. Got eight new shots of something," he commented. Redeemer wasted no time in dashing to the water's edge sniffing at the air as though he smelt something familiar. Bryce looked on, watching as the bear cub rose on its hind legs and glared out across the pool to the other side. Looking in the same direction, he himself saw nothing.

Even as he used his 35mm camera and a telephoto lens, he still saw nothing. Redeemer however was showing signs of fear and aggression. "What the heck do you see little guy? I can't see a thing." Finally the cub went back onto all fours and traipsed back to his side. "I guess whatever you saw is gone eh?" he responded as the cub slumped to the ground and rolled over onto his back.

"We'll be on our way in a minute so don't be taking one of your cub naps. I only have the tripod and camera to put away then we'll head for home. It'll be getting near dusk by the time we get there, and some hot grub will top the day off." Wrestling with the tripod, he pinched his finger with it when it collapsed. He hated when that happened, and he silently cursed.

"All right, all set," he grabbed the pack and rifle. "Come on, let's head for home." Two hours later and no worse for wear, but tired, they coursed their way back to camp. Redeemer went directly to his sweater, falling asleep even before Bryce got the gear and camera's put away. He was showing signs of weariness a mile or so earlier and he'd slowed down quite a bit. Once the smell of camp was evident to him, the cub picked up his pace. Now, he was totally drained. His body twitched involuntarily as he slept.

Bryce sat down at the table and sighed. He was tired as

well, but it was only nearing 6:00 or 7:00 p.m., and he didn't want to go to sleep yet. There were still a few hours of daylight left, the sun was only starting to set. Running his hand across his chin, he decided he'd put the solar heated shower out back of his tent to a fourth test since being there. He'd even put on a clean pair of under shorts and socks, the ones he wore now were taking on a smell all their own. He sniffed under his armpit, *Wheweee, the shirt has got to go too,* he exhaled and gulped for a breath of fresh air. *I haven't stunk like that since the last time I needed a shower.* Snickering he shook his head.

An hour later, showered, shaved and wearing cleaner clothes, he heated up what was left of the coffee. He threw together a meal for both himself and Redeemer, who by now was full of piss and vinegar and was giving him a rough time by getting into everything, including knocking over the woodpile. "You're a crazy little bear, you know that," Bryce commented as he stood up and stacked the woodpile. Turning in the nick of time, he stopped the cub from climbing onto the table and knocking everything off.

"Hold up there, little bear," he said with a halting voice. "You can't be going up there. Come on, get down." The bear bolted between his legs, almost knocking him over. He ran around the tent and back again, chased his shadow and ran head long into a table leg, which knocked him back. Redeemer shook his head a couple of times, obviously he felt it, and Bryce chuckled. "See horsing around and not paying attention can get you into trouble."

Redeemer looked at him then meandered over to his sweater. "Wore out again are you? I sure hope so, don't think I could keep up with you. Going to have to go on longer walks I guess, hey little bear?" Redeemer rolled to his back, staring up at the tent awning then, ever so slowly, his eyes closed.

Pouring a coffee, Bryce reminisced, deciding he'd take the time in the next day to upload everything onto his laptop. It would be a day spent at camp and catching up. He might take Redeemer for a short walk later in the day, but not until his work was done. There were three memory cards of photos to go through, plus a bunch of hand written notes, which could probably use some editing, and sorting out.

One thing he didn't like about his elected career was when he started to get behind on paper work. He dreaded that. It seemed to bother him the most when he was out in the field. Back home on his acreage, he had stacks of paper work, some as old as nine or ten months, folders and files here and there were stacked on chairs and tucked into boxes marked *urgent* or *whatever,* the latter, obviously being less important. Out here though, he always tried to stay focused and organised. There was a point to everything he did in the field, and this was likely why he concentrated on staying on top of the paperwork. Back home at Parkview Valley, it didn't seem as important.

He lived in a modest four-bedroom house on a nice fifty-acre lot of evergreen, poplar and a mass of cedar trees. There was one road leading to his house and one road leaving. It was the perfect place other than the mountains. Through his land ran the Beaver Creek, the Hudu Creek, and an old pioneer wagon trail he'd been working on fixing up.

He always found things along the trail, like old empty cans, two broken wagon wheels, and parts and pieces of an old wagon that was said to have belonged to a family that used the trail. The story was they all perished along the trail as they coursed their way east. How true the story was, he didn't know. He did know with certain authority however, that the wagon trail was indeed used by pioneers going both east to the prairies, and west to the pacific coast.

How many used the trail couldn't be guessed, as there were easier routes, which even back then were likely used more frequently. Swallowing the last of his coffee, he rose, traipsed over to the tent and entered. Sitting down at the workstation, he organised the memory cards and notes he'd go through in the morning, laying them out in chronological order, or in order of importance. There was a lot of stuff to thumb through, he noted, as he looked on. Rising now from his workstation, he tossed his belt and hunting knife onto the desk, and retreated to his cot. Stretching out, he listened to a pair of loons chorusing on the lake. The symphony relaxed him, and in a few minutes he was sound asleep.

Chapter 7

Bryce found himself tossing and turning most of the night. He awoke the next morning at 5:00 a.m. Not even the sun was yet visible. There were a few stars twinkling as he prepared his morning coffee. He couldn't recall the last time he had awakened so early. It made little difference. An early start is all it meant.

He booted up his laptop, plugged in the digital camera, and uploaded the pictures he'd taken over the past few days. He spent some time editing a few of the pictures, turning his focus onto the pile of notes and data he gathered during the same amount of time. A conglomerate of notes and graphs of foliage and wildlife growth is what it all added up to, but he went at it headlong. Finally, taking a break after nearly an hour, he stepped outside.

The morning air felt exhilarating as he inhaled deeply and wiped his brow. He was surprised Redeemer was sacked out inside, but then again the little bear had given its all the day before. Tossing some recently cooked potatoes and carrots into Redeemer's pot, as well as two cans of salmon and a handful of dried apricots, he called to the cub. "Hey, got something for you, and if you don't eat it, I might be tempted to eat it myself."

The cub poked his head out of the tent, looking in the direction to where Bryce was kneeling. Sniffing the air, the cub snorted a muffled sound as he drew close to the pot and Bryce. "Good morning. Come one dig in, no more snacks until lunchtime." He turned back to the table, poured a coffee, and ate three sticks of jerky and a handful of the same dried apricots he'd given Redeemer.

"I was thinking, later when we go for our walk, we ought to keep our eyes peeled for an old rotten stump. I'll show you the grubs and stuff a fellow like you, heck even a fellow like me, can eat. Bears and me, we eat them all the time," he chuckled. "I don't think it'll hurt you any to learn that at this stage of the game. You have to learn that animal instinct. It might save you sometime."

43

He lifted his cup of coffee, and took a drink. "I have more work to catch up on. Don't go getting into mischief. I'll be inside." Entering the tent with his coffee in hand, he returned to the pile of notes and graphs. "Ho hum and a bottle of rum." he said as he sat down and opened the note pad to the place where he'd left off.

For four hours he toiled with and edited all the notes, feeling relieved when he finally finished the task. Stepping outside to check up on Redeemer, he was glad to find that he hadn't travelled far and was down near the canoe. "Whatcha doing there, little fellow?" Redeemer looked at him and bound toward him, tripping over his own feet and somersaulting. Finally making the distance, he rubbed against his shins.

"Glad you stuck close by. I figure that deserves a nice thick piece of jerky." Walking the short distance to the food cache, Bryce opened the big heavy lid and grabbed a bag of jerky and a few other items. "There that ought to keep us fed for the rest of the day," he commented as he secured the lid and locked it. "Come on, let's get back to the tent. I'll give you a piece once we get there." Finding a thicker piece of the jerked meat once he finally sat down at the table, he tossed it to Redeemer, who gleefully enjoyed the treat.

By 6:00 p.m., the tasks he'd set aside to do that day, including cataloguing the photos, were accomplished. Stepping out into the cool evening, he looked around for Redeemer, shocked to see that the bear cub had somehow ended up in the canoe and was now afloat out on the lake. Shaking his head, he darted to the shore. "How did you manage that?" The cub looked in the direction of the shore, and although he was a distance away, it was easy to tell he was calling for help. Bryce had little choice but go for an early evening swim.

Removing his boots and outer clothing, he stepped into the cold lake, wading out until it was waist deep then he took a deep breath and dived in. He swam the distance to where the canoe and Redeemer sat idle. The canoe bobbed this way and that, as he pulled himself onboard, only to find that the oars were not inside. "Looks like I'll be paddling this vessel with my hands. How did you ever manage to dislodge this canoe?" he questioned, as he began stroking the water.

Redeemer showed his gratitude by climbing all over Bryce, finally tipping the canoe over. It was comical in a sense, but Redeemer didn't think so, he still hadn't learned how to swim. He cried out in fear as he splashed about trying to keep his head above the water. It took only a few seconds for him to learn, and in less time than it took to put the canoe upright, he was swimming for shore.

Pulling himself back into the canoe, Bryce watched for a few minutes, as the bear cub smoothly swam toward shore like an Olympic swimmer. It was quite the distance to swim, and had been tough on him. Noting that Redeemer's strokes were getting weaker, and that shore was still a few yards away, Bryce madly paddled with his hands, soon pulling up alongside the cub.

Grabbing him by the scruff of the neck, he hoisted the overexerted cub into the canoe. "Now don't be moving around too much; we don't want to go in the drink again. I'd say you passed your first swimming lesson, though. You swam quite the distance for a little fellow. For now, sit there in the middle and relax; we're almost to shore."

The cub didn't budge. He lay flat out on the bottom of the canoe like a sack of potatoes. A few minutes later stepping onto the shore, Bryce docked the canoe. His body temperature had risen from the rapid paddling, and the warm evening breeze felt salutary as it gently blew.

"This is the end of the road. We're on solid ground again, come on hop out." Bryce coaxed. Redeemer rose and baled over the side darting directly for camp. Bryce decided to maroon the canoe. Picking up his clothes and boots he headed back to camp, finding Redeemer zonked out on the old sweater.

Tossing one of his boots at the sleeping cub, startled him. The cub jumped up and took a stance, sniffing at the boot that had so rudely wakened him. "So how did you like your first canoe ride? You could say one good thing came about, you at least learned to swim," Bryce said as he looked on.

In the blink of an eye Redeemer grabbed the boot and darted around the side of the tent. Bryce chased after him, knowing full well if the bear cub wanted to, he could easily wreck the boot, and they were the only ones he brought on this trip. He caught up to him and retrieved the boot, which luckily enough only suffered some teeth marks. "Sheesh, lucky I caught up. You were going to wreck it weren't you?"

He chuckled at the look Redeemer shot him. "Imagine that, you were besmirched by a boot, little fellow. I didn't mean to startle you that badly. Sorry little buddy." Turning with boot in hand, he walked back around the tent and dressed. Redeemer darted back to the tent and as quickly, knocked over the woodpile for the second time in as many days. Bryce was still dressing, turning to look at all the commotion. Redeemer was routing through the scattered wood as though he was on the trail of something, and in a few minutes, he had a field mouse in his grasp. He tossed it this way and that, watching as it scooted into some nearby shrubbery and out of sight.

"That was what all that was about eh? Cool, you have a good instinct. Except, I think the idea is to eat what you hunt down, *that* of course meaning *game only*, and only when you are *hungry*." Standing, Bryce walked over to the woodpile and began to re-stack it. The whole time the cub desperately pawed at his feet and boots, trying to kill them.

"Look, you aren't going to get my boots, so back off little guy, come on, enough," he complained as he stacked the wood, gently kicking at Redeemer. He was smiling as he stood, tossing the last piece of wood onto the pile. "What am I going to do with you? I already told you my boots aren't for you. Get now, go on… go find something else to chew on like a big log or something." Bryce walked back to the table. Redeemer darted under it, continuing to be a pest to Bryce's boots and feet, pawing and gnawing them like they were animals that needed to be taught a lesson.

Bryce couldn't bring himself to discipline Redeemer. It was his own fault for tossing the boot at him in the first place. He shook his head, taking a pen and paper he wrote down. *One pair of Koflach hiking boots or equivalent- size' eleven and a half. One pair of hiking shoes Spalding or other type, same size.* "There I'll get Jackson to deliver these to me with the grub order. I don't think the ones on my feet got much hope in surviving the summer, and I could certainly use a pair of *hiking shoes* anyway." He continued to gently kick at Redeemer, who was under the table still pawing and gnawing at his feet. He was grateful the bear's bite was weak. It was more of an annoyance than anything else.

During the course of kicking at the little beast, he must have kicked a bit too hard or stepped on his foot. The cub let out a muffled cry and growl then shot from underneath the table and directly into the tent. It was a good thing he hadn't zipped it closed. Redeemer would have torn through the flap, likely causing the entire tent to collapse.

Wanting to make sure the cub was all right, he stood from the table, but hadn't made three steps before Redeemer bolted out of the tent with feathers from a pillow trailing behind him like falling snow. "No, no you crazy bear," he said as he chased after him to reclaim what was left of his pillow. A brief tug of war ensued, and the pillow ripped completely in half, causing them both to fall back a few steps as the opposition released.

Bryce stood there dumbfounded, and poor Redeemer looked on as though he knew exactly what he'd done. Bryce couldn't help but to break out in laughter, which in turn caused the cub to run in circles and go goofy.

"You know," Bryce began as he caught his breath, kneeling down to Redeemer's level, "you know you are a vengeful fellow. That was my only pillow." He smiled as the cub darted toward him and began licking his face with his rough tongue. Redeemer's wet nose dabbed his face, causing him to start laughing all over again. They wrestled for a half-hour or so, until finally Bryce stood up, "All right, all right that's enough. Playtime is over. Let's go see what we can throw together for supper. You made me work up an appetite."

After feasting, and a fresh pot of coffee was perked to top it all off, Bryce was satisfied with his day's accomplishments. He was now caught up on his obligated paper work and documentation that he'd fallen behind on, and things were good. Putting his hands behind his head, he stretched out his feet. "Hey, Redeemer, if you were a person, would you classify tomorrow as mid-week?" he questioned with as much thought as humor.

"Cause you know what, if tomorrow is mid-week, we've been promised another visit by Rayne-Bow Foxeagle, that beautiful enchantress of Toby Creek." He went silent as he thought of her. Redeemer looked over at him once from his curled up position on the sweater then tucked his head and resumed with a deserved forty winks.

Bryce listened to the evening as it came to life. Frogs croaked, crickets hummed, and loons sung out. In the distance a coyote yelped in hope of getting a reply, an audible, 'whooohooo' echoed nearby as grandfather owl made his presence known. Bryce took all the sounds in, noting how there was nothing sweeter than the sound of a forest as night loomed, turning day to dusk and dusk to nightfall. "Home sweet home," he whispered.

Chapter 8

Rising with the sun that morning, his hope was that Rayne would stop by with good news about Hector. She commented she'd return mid-week, with news that old Hector had or hadn't returned. Either way, she was expected. Bryce could only hope that she would bear good news. Dressing, he exited the tent, sitting at the table, he felt refreshed and exhilarated. It was another warm morning.

There was a symphony of birds chirping and whistling so grand, that he couldn't help but feel good. Their songs echoed across Leroy Lake and through the surrounding woods, like a symphony never heard. Their stage was the forest. He hadn't heard that many chorusing since arriving in March. Spring was definitely making itself present. He sipped at his coffee while the symphony continued. Redeemer finally joined him, sprawling out on the ground next to the table, anxiously licking his chops while waiting for his breakfast.

"Let me guess, it's time for some grub." Bryce tossed some food together for Redeemer. "Another gourmet meal my friend, straight from Bryce's kitchen into your stomach." He set the pot of food down. "Everything to make you grow up big and strong. Potatoes, veggies, some dried fruit and oatmeal, dried egg powder and some dehydrated milk dust, which I like to call it, all topped off with a can of salmon. Mmm, sounds good." At least Redeemer seemed to think so.

Bryce patted him, and for the first time noticed how the cub had gone through a growing spurt over the last few days. "Redeemer, did you grow another inch or two over night? Looks like you've gained some height and weight." he commented as he looked at the cub. "I guess I'm doing something right. You are growing." In a few gulps and chews, the mound of food set out for Redeemer diminished like a sandcastle being washed away by choppy waters. "Feel better now big-little guy." He poured himself a second coffee. "Today, we're going to start off with a walk. We can't go far. The enchantress of Toby Creek might show up and I'd hate to miss her. We'll stay close. I'll finish my coffee then we'll be off like a herd of turtles."

Redeemer wasn't content on waiting lazily in the sun; he was as anxious as a two- year old child in a candy store, full of excitement and curiosity of what the day might bring. It was hard keeping the cub in view, as the two walked firstly along the shore and then into the south-west woods, and Bryce gave up on trying to do so. Instead, he let the cub roam freely. He never wandered far. Every ten minutes or so, he would show himself or Bryce would stumble across him routing through an old log or stump.

He was moved that Redeemer was using some of his basic bear instincts. It told him that the cub was growing in more ways than in leaps and bounds. The cub would not have survived, he knew, if he hadn't intervened. It was a decision that would forever change the course of Redeemer's life. It saddened him somewhat, knowing that because of his intervention, the cub would never live a normal bear's life. Yet, had he not intervened, the cub would have likely joined his mother by now. There would be a hefty permit fee and likely a ton of legalities and red tape to go through before he could legally accommodate Redeemer, even if for only a few years.

Pulling up to an old fallen log, he sat down. Redeemer was within his view and he watched the cub with admiration. Redeemer glanced over to where he sat and he galloped to his side, knowing if Bryce was sitting down, snacks were going to be served.

Reaching down, Bryce scratched Redeemer under his chin. "I figure we've hiked a good three miles. I got some photos of a few different birds plus a bunch of madly growing foliage. Not to mention a few quick pictures of a squirrel, as well as a racoon we passed that was hanging out on a tree branch a mile or so back. Not bad I'd say, for a short walk. Spring has definitely sprung; now if we could only get a few photos of the bear in this area as well as the elusive mountain caribou; that would be a real treat. In time I suppose." He reminisced how great it would be if he did indeed photograph a few of the caribou.

THE COALITION OF PURGATORY

Looking back at Redeemer, he smiled. "I guess you'd like a snack? All right." Rooting around in his pack, Bryce pulled out a couple pieces of jerky and a bag of dried fruit. He tossed Redeemer the jerky first and the cub gnawed and chewed for a few minutes. When he swallowed the last of the meat, Bryce handed him a handful of the dried fruit from the bag he'd opened. It was apple. Redeemer sniffed at the offering. It was a new scent to him, a bit tart and sweet all at once.

"This is green apple. We haven't had one of these yet. Go on take it, Redeemer, it's good for you." He tried to coax Redeemer to try a piece. Redeemer held fast, waiting until Bryce finally ate some himself. He lay down sniffing it at first, pushing it with his nose until finally deciding that it did smell good, and finished it off. "See not so bad." They shared what was left of the bag. Feeling revived from the snack, they rose. "I say we turn around here and head back to camp. Rayne may be on her way by now. Come on, let's head back." With Redeemer at his heels, they coursed their way back to camp.

As sure as the sun sets in the west, Rayne, true to her word, showed up at camp just before dusk. The news she brought wasn't good. There still hadn't been any sign of Hector. "Do you know of the places he might go?" Bryce asked with concern, as he poured her a coffee.

"Yes, and I've been to some of those places. He hasn't been to any of the secret places he's shown me. On occasion, he spoke of a place called Muskrat Creek, but I haven't a clue on where that might be. Nor was I able to find it on any of the maps he has pinned to the wall. I don't know if I should be worried, or if Grandfather will show up tomorrow." Rayne took the coffee from him and sipped at it as she contemplated.

"Muskrat Creek?" he questioned. "I don't think I've even heard of that place. Is it supposed to be around here?"

"As far as I know. It's a place where he speaks to the departed. You know the spirits of our elders and such. I have no idea where this place is," Rayne responded as she took another sip from her coffee. Bryce too sipped from his cup in deep contemplation.

"Maybe we should try and find this place. If it is around here, I can't imagine it being too hard to find. There are a couple of small lakes ten miles east of here, with creeks flowing out of them. I figure that'd be within walking distance. What say you?" Bryce looked intently at Rayne while he waited for her response.

"That would be a good idea. I don't think we would be wise however to leave for those lakes at this time of day. I can be back here in the morning tomorrow, say seven-ish."

"Why not spend the night? There is plenty of room. I don't mind sleeping on the floor with Redeemer. You could sleep on the cot. I do have fresh linen."

Rayne looked coyly at Bryce. "What kind of a girl do you think I am?" she asked with humor.

"I think you're a perfectly wonderful person. My intent isn't to put any moves on you." he responded, feeling a bit embarrassed.

"And why not?" Rayne questioned teasingly.

Taken back at her response he felt awkward. "Umm, I mean I'm not trying to…to umm, you know get you in the sack. I only figure it would be easier to head out in the morning if you stayed the night."

Rayne began to laugh. "I know what your intent was. I was funning with you. It would be easier if I stayed, and as long as you promise to be a gentleman, I will stay."

"Very well. I do promise to be a gentleman. It'll be nice to have a roommate even if for only one night. Your company will be a real treat." Bryce brought his cup to his lips and swallowed the last of his coffee. "Would you like a refill?" he asked as he rose and poured himself another cup.

"Yes, please. I do love camp coffee," she said, handing Bryce her cup. He filled it and handed it back.

"I agree. Camp coffee appeals to my palate as well."

The remainder of the evening passed slowly. The two friends took another walk along the lake, and as with the first time he and Rayne met, the two of them looked westerly at the falling sun. Again, another beautiful sunset was painted across the horizon, and the two gazed upon it in deep thought. Finally returning to camp, Bryce lit a fire and they conversed until the darkening sky was pitch black and the sunset was all but a memory. Retrieving the clean linen, he fitted the cot with the fresh sheets. "Well, the cot is all fixed up for you. If you want to hit the sack feel free," he said to her as he exited the tent. Instead they sat outside, talking for another hour before deciding it was time to sleep.

Chapter 9

Waking early the next morning, Bryce tiptoed out of the tent, looking around in the predawn for Redeemer, who usually came running for his morning feeding the moment the old Coleman stove was fired up. Today however, Redeemer was tardy, and he wondered where the cub might be.

The sound of laughing confirmed the cub was inside the tent. Rising from his chair, he entered. Redeemer was gnawing and clawing Rayne's long jet-black hair, hanging over the side of the cot. She was laughing and cooing as the cub rolled around on his back like a professional break-dancer, biting the long strands of hair that dangled only a few inches from the floor.

"A little playful this morning, are we?" he asked as he laughed at the cub's antics. His presence made Redeemer dart around the room this way and that, and in his haste, he crashed into the legs of the cot, which caused it to collapse.

Rayne laughed and screamed all at once, as she slid off the cot and onto the floor naked. Bryce could hardly contain himself as Redeemer dashed between his legs, heading for the outdoors. Chuckling he helped Rayne up off the floor. She was in hysterics and laughing so hard tears rolled down her cheeks. "Sorry about that. I've never seen him act that nutty before." Draping a blanket over Rayne's shoulder, he bent down to look at the damage done to the legs of the cot.

"No need to for an apology. I quite enjoyed that little bit of entertainment. It's not everyday one gets to see a grizzly cub up close, let alone play with one."

"Yeah, he is a bit of a rascal. He gets into playful moods and can't contain himself long enough to make a fair judgement on the damage he can cause. I imagine by the time I'm done here, all I'll have left is the tent," he replied as he chuckled. "As long as he didn't hurt you any, I don't suppose any harm has been done. He did make a mess of the cot legs though. I'll likely have to put a few pieces of wood under the end so it will sit level, otherwise it might as well be a big Lazyboy," he said as he rose. "By the way, good morning.

Coffee is brewing, and if you like I can throw together some pancakes."

"That would be super. Thank you." Nodding he gave Rayne the once over before he exited, smiling the entire time. Outside and under the picnic table, Redeemer had again got a hold of Bryce's hiking boot, and by now had gnawed the entire back off. Pieces of the once Koflach hiking boot were strewn around the bear cub in an array of grey and red coloured rubber and plastic. Bryce shook his head as he reached down to grab what was left of the boot. Redeemer however had different plans, snatching the boot away then running behind the tent, with Bryce close on his heels.

"Redeemer, Redeemer, you little bugger," he yelled after him as he set chase. "Get back here with my boot." Finally catching up with the cub, he tackled him, and the two of them rolled around on the saturated dew covered ground until finally Bryce was victorious. Holding the boot above his head like the Olympic torch, he did a little dance. "And the winner is..." he began as he got a glimpse of Rayne standing nearby, shaking her head. She looked at the two of them like they were both nuts.

"By the look of that boot, I'd say the bear wins." Rayne said as she began to laugh.

Bryce lowered the boot from above his head, and looked at it. "I suppose so, eh. There isn't enough boot here for me to wear." he comically said as he approached her, Redeemer fast at his side. "The thing is they're the only boots I got, until my next supply shipment. I'm going to have to make it work somehow."

"Perhaps we should make a brief stop at my Grandfather's cabin. I'm certain he has a pair of boots that would fit you. If not he has many pairs of moccasins, I'm sure we'll find something. Now where are those pancakes?" Rayne asked with humour, her hands on her hips.

"Yes indeed." The two walked back to the table, and finished the last of their breakfast and coffee before they mounted Rayne's horse and headed for Hector's cabin ten miles away. Redeemer ran alongside, slowing every now and again to sniff the air and his surroundings. Never though, did the cub lose sight of them. An hour later they strode up to the cabin and dismounted. Things hadn't changed since Bryce was there last, and as he tied the horse to the horse rail, the front door swung open, and low and behold, there stood Hector. "Grandfather!" Rayne exclaimed, "where have you been? I've been worried."

"I have been to the sacred place. I've had visions of deceit and greed. The white man who wishes to change this place into his own vision, will lie to all of us to make his dream a reality. He will be hard to stop. Not even the white men who oppose him, will be able to stop his destruction. The forefathers tell me this in the visions." Hector grew silent for a moment then continued. "There is no more need to fight."

"Hang on, Hector, we aren't going to give up the fight, not now, not ever. Ottawa has not yet approved any of his ideas. There is still time to convince them. It doesn't go for final deliberation until September."

"Yes. As we speak now, he is preparing to make his move. I will travel to Ottawa myself in the coming weeks and make a plea for my people. This, I know, has once already been done. Yet the plans to destroy this place go uninterrupted. Your work here, Bryce, is good work that, in time, may very well be the one reason that your people in Ottawa will listen." Hector inhaled deeply, "I must make the journey to Ottawa and make my plea. The forefathers have also convinced me of this. Now please both of you, come and sit with me on the back porch. We will drink coffee and talk of better things. I see that you wear only one boot. Why is that?" Hector asked with confusion.

Rayne chuckled as she explained the reason. A smile crossed old Hector's face as he listened. "Yes. Indeed, I have a pair of moccasins that have not yet been worn, and will surely fit your feet. Come." Hector turned and walked back into his cabin. Both Rayne and Bryce followed together. "These moccasins are the ones I spoke of," Hector began as he held up the pair. "I double stitched them to make them strong. They are made from deer hide, should last you throughout your stay here in these mountains." Bryce took the pair, thanking Hector as he slipped them on. He was surprised at how well they fit his feet. It was as though they were made to fit him exactly.

"They sure feel good. Thank you very much. I was afraid I'd have to wait until my supply shipment came in before I'd have footwear again." He walked around the cabin admiring the workmanship of the handcrafted moccasins.

"I'm glad they make your feet happy," Hector replied as he smiled. "Now let us retreat to the back porch. Rayne, please bring the coffee." Hector slipped out the back door and sat down at the round table. Bryce sat across from him, admiring the view of the valley and mountain peaks of the Purgatory Mountains in the distance. Like the moccasins on his feet, the mountains and all its valleys and lakes were a work of art. It was hard to grasp that perhaps one day he would be looking across the draw at a ski resort. The thought annoyed him and tugged at his heartstrings. *What a waste it will all be,* he thought as he continued to gaze at the mountain across the way.

Finally the back door opened and Rayne walked over to the table, setting down the coffee and condiments. "Here is the coffee," she said as she sat next to Hector, averting her own gaze out across the draw and toward the mountains. Hector poured each of them a cup and sipping his hot brew he smiled.

"I see that we are not alone." He pointed his chin toward Redeemer, who was curiously digging in an old rotten log. "Watch him closely and you will learn wisdom from him. He will become your brother, unattached by his world. He has been granted a new life, and it will be up to you, Bryce, to assure his success. A big task for one man alone."

"You couldn't be more right. It will indeed be a big task. Nevertheless, I'm committed to him. Sometimes I wonder though, if my decision to take him under my wing was a bad decision. Then again, I think of what could have become of him hadn't I stepped in. At least now, he has a new lease on life. Like you said," he replied as he looked over to the bear cub.

Hector sat in silence, sipping his coffee and nodding. By mid-day, and after a few hours visiting with Hector, Rayne and Bryce were making their way back to Leroy Lake, Redeemer nipping at their heels. "It is sure good to know Hector is all right. He didn't say much though while we visited, did he?" Bryce questioned.

"No. It concerns me too. Grandfather is usually more outspoken. Perhaps he is tired from his journey. I will know more after he has napped. I am glad he is home. No more worries for now. This trip he says he has planned for Ottawa, concerns me." Rayne responded as she heeled her horse's flank getting the animal to speed up.

"Why?"

"He once told me that he would only leave these mountains to avenge its destruction. I can only imagine what it is he has planned."

"You surely don't think he has plans to hurt anyone. Do you?" Bryce couldn't fathom that idea. There was a long silence as Rayne waited to respond.

"Grandfather has sworn to protect this place. He is capable of many things, killing another man to protect what he believes to be sacred, is certainly something he is capable of doing. Will he do such a thing? Only Grandfather knows. If I knew for sure what his intent was, I couldn't stop him without first hog-tying him. Perhaps that is exactly what I will do," Rayne sullenly said with sincerity.

"Please, do not be discouraged if I do not stop by for a while. I must stay close to Grandfather. I must convince him that his trip to Ottawa is not necessary. I mustn't leave him alone." Rayne heeled her old buck horse again as they crested the last incline before Bryce's camp, they were close enough now that Redeemer wouldn't get lost, and looking behind, Bryce could see the bear cub as it too began the last jaunt to camp at full speed. Rayne's horse finally came to a stop short of the tent, and he dismounted.

"Thank you for the ride back. I'll see you again soon, and don't be hesitant to swing by anytime if you need help with Hector." He winked as he smiled up at Rayne; she was a sight of sheer beauty sitting on that horse. Smiling back, Rayne turned and galloped off. He watched as she disappeared into the forest. Walking over to the table he sat in contemplation, his mind raced with all that had been said. He knew that Hector indeed swore to kill the first man who stuck a spade into the sacred land of his people, but he didn't want to believe it.

By now, Redeemer made his way back to camp. As soon as he saw Bryce sitting at the table, he bolted toward him, and in one crashing leap he toppled him onto the ground, licking his face as though he'd been lost forever. "Whoa, there little buddy. What is that all about?" he playfully wrestled with the cub. Redeemer rose on his hind legs, roaring as ferociously as his little lungs would let him.

It was as though he was giving him the '*what for*' for leaving him in the dust. "I see. You are a little mad that we sped off. Rayne was in a bit of a hurry. Besides, I knew you'd find your way home. After all you are a bear aren't you?" Redeemer tilted his head and went back onto all fours then sauntered over to his food dish.

Standing up, Bryce dusted himself off. "Give me a minute and I'll get food into your dish." The cub looked at him, sighing heavily as he lay down beside his dish, waiting patiently for it to be filled. Grabbing the pot, Bryce looked at the leftovers from that mornings pancake feast, there were a half dozen cold pancakes and some sausage still in the big cast iron frying pan. He added these to the pot along with two cans of salmon. "How does this look? It looks good enough for me to eat," he commented, as he set the pot down next to the cub. Redeemer didn't even wait to smell the food, finishing it in a few big gulps.

"You certainly have a healthy appetite. I don't think even a full- grown man could have eaten all that as quickly as you did. That's all right, though, I don't expect your appetite to stay pocket size. It is going to keep growing, just like you." he remarked as he turned and walked back to the table. The stars in the sky were dim due to the emerging pallid yellow moon.

Putting his hands behind his neck, Bryce stretched out his legs and looked to the darkening sky. It had been an interesting day, although he hadn't got any work done, he was glad he spent it with Rayne and old Hector. He was grateful for the moccasins as well, which he now looked at with admiration. Hector had done an excellent job on them, and they felt good on his feet. They were the first pair he'd ever worn, but they would certainly not be the last pair he owned.

Dumping what was left of his coffee onto the ground, he rose and picked up a couple pieces of wood before entering the tent. He was tired and sleep was calling him. First, he had to fix the cot. Redeemer followed behind him, taking his place on the floor. Curling up he closed his eyes and was soon fast asleep.

Bryce smiled at the cub as he walked over to him, scratching him behind the ear. "It was a busy day for you as well, eh? Tomorrow we have to catch up on what we missed today, but that's tomorrow, sleep well little buddy." He set the wood he carried down at the end of the cot, placing it under the one end that no longer had legs, due to Redeemer's little escapade. "Yeah, that will work." He shook the cot to make sure it was sturdy, removed his moccasins and clothes, and slipped beneath the covers.

Chapter 10

The day started off like any other, the only difference being that he could hear the sound of a chainsaw. Although faint as it was, it was definitely a chainsaw. Retrieving his binoculars, he scoured the perimeter of Leroy Lake, but he saw nothing. Focusing now on the north-east mountain road, he could make out four white-trucks and men scattered here and there on the ridge above the road. Obviously, they were 4x4's and likely company vehicles. *Wonder what that is all about,* he thought as he sipped from his coffee.

Taking up the binoculars again, he gazed once more up on the ridge to where he had spotted the first man. From his camp, and because of the distance, he couldn't make out much more than the fact that there were men and trucks up that way. *Best have a look see.* Gathering his gear, he called for Redeemer. "Hey Redeemer, are you up for a hike? Looks like we have some kind of activity going on up in the north-east ridge. I figure it's a good day's hike from here; we'll likely be staying outdoors tonight." The cub rubbed up against his shins, and made a muffled snorting sound, as if to say, "Come on, let's go."

Reaching down, Bryce scratched the cub behind his ear. "Good, good. I'm glad you're all for it. Just got to double check everything and we'll be off." Checking over his gear, he made sure he had what they would need to spend a night out in the forest. Satisfied, he grabbed his .308 and an extra clip, and the pair headed north-east. The first few miles of the hike was time consuming and dreadful. The forest was thick with jack pine and scattered with frozen patches, and the snow was knee deep. It was indeed rugged and untouched, although deadly as it was, it was as peaceful as any country he'd seen.

Resting near a mountain stream, its edges still frozen, Bryce spoke softly to the cub. "Some nice country here, eh?" He looked around. Redeemer was lapping at the cold water, relishing every thirst-quenching gulp. In the distance they could hear the din of a chainsaw. "Sounds like we're getting closer. I'm not sure if it's Robertar & Robertar's men. Could be I'm wrong though, and as sure as the sun sets in the west, it is. We'll have to wait and see to be sure." There was a long pause as Bryce looked toward the ridge, but could see nothing from where they sat. "Well, figure we should continue. We've had a good half-hour break, and I'm itching to find out what those men are doing. Come on, time is slipping away," he said as he stood, with his rifle in hand. "We still have a half-mile to hike before we'll get any answers."

Back at Hector Foxeagle's cabin near Toby Creek, an argument was ensuing between Hector and Rayne-Bow. "I do not think it is a good idea that you go to Ottawa, Grandfather. It is miles away and big at that. A lot could go wrong."

"There is nothing more wrong then what that man, Robertar and his associates have planned for this sacred land of the Ktunaxa. I will not be stopped, Rayne. The forefathers have said so," Hector responded, as he looked out across the draw between Toby Creek and the Purgatory Mountains; but he knew she was right. Ottawa was miles away, and a lot could go wrong. However, he was adamant that he needed to go. Perhaps his words could at least prolong the devastation that would undoubtedly come to the Purgatory Mountains.

If nothing else, he had to try, and try he would. Breaking his gaze of the mountains, Hector looked into Rayne's eyes. "As a child you played in this forest. As a woman, you visited this sacred place. Is it not a shame that one day it all may be lost, to some bigwig whose hunger for money and power outweighs his common sense?"

"Yes it is. If I could single handily put a stop to it, I most certainly would. It is a shame, and I'm certain disaster will follow if indeed Robertar gets his wish. For now let those who have the power to prevent it, do their work." Rayne responded as the air became still. The silence of the mountains brought a calming effect, as both Hector and Rayne stood in self-contemplation, their gaze again averted toward the forest-clad mountains.

For a few brief moments, Rayne thought back to her childhood. She'd spent a lot of time in and amongst the illustrious mountain range that she now looked at. The thought that someday she'd instead be looking at a five star ski resort, pulled at her heartstrings, as memories of her past fluttered by. "I see by your eyes that your memories of this place are great," Hector drew in a deep breath. "It will be a kiss of death to these mountains and all it protects, once the destruction for construction begins."

Rayne sighed in half agreement, "That is why it is imperative that we do not give up hope. There is a chance, that further plans to transform this place, will be denied by the Canadian Government. It will be a catastrophe if they don't."

Fifteen miles to the north-east, Bryce, and Redeemer were making their final ascent to the ridge. The muffled voices of the men above them were more audible as the two crept closer. Bryce wanted to be certain that the men weren't a threat before he introduced himself. Holding tightly to Redeemer's neck, he got the cub to lie down. The two of them crouched as they listened intently to the men's conversation.

"It doesn't matter, Clayburgh. I want you to back up this truck. There is no way we're going to make it any further."

"What do ya suppose old Roberto Robertar is going to say when we tell him we could only make it this far? He is going to flip his lid, is what he's going to do."

"Like I said, Clayburgh, it doesn't matter. Turn your rig around, if you still want to be employed tomorrow."

It was clear that the workers were from the Robertar & Robertar Land Development Company, and the man barking the orders was obviously the foreman. Likely they were attempting to get some early surveying done, but were not very well equipped. Bryce wasn't surprised that two of the four trucks were stuck, chuckling to himself, he listened as truck doors slammed and men hollered. The sound of spinning tires and heaving men, echoed through the wood like a loud Three Stooges film. The scent of hot rubber was an after effect, lingering in the air as the last truck finally got its grip, spun around and followed suit as all four trucks began the descent along the rugged mountain road.

Bryce rose, dusting the snow from the seat of his pants

as he looked up toward the road. "Sheesh, never even had the time to introduce myself," he commented with sarcasm. "Come on lets go have a look see at where those lug heads got stuck. They were Robertar's men undoubtedly. Can't believe they'd attempt getting up his far. They should've figured out that this road isn't ready to be driven on. Heck, it's still covered in snow and God-awful muddy underneath. Another month maybe, before she'll be dry enough to travel on."

He ambled over to where the trucks had been stuck. "They sure chewed up this area. Just for fun, I'm going to snap a few stills. A picture is worth a thousand words, or so they say. What words the pictures will say about this, is beyond me." Shrugging his shoulders, he began taking pictures.

The cub was a short distance away in the other ruts and mud pit caused by the last truck. He was sniffing at a puddle of bright green liquid. To the young cub, it was a sweet scent, much like honey, and he lapped at it. Before Bryce realised what Redeemer was doing, the bear cub had lapped up most of the liquid. "No Redeemer," Bryce said sharply, shooing the bear away from the puddle. Scooping some of the green tainted snow into an empty film container so it could be analysed later if need be. He quickly took a few pictures of the green liquid as it slowly melted away the ice and soaked into mud. Racing to the cub's side he shoved two of his fingers down Redeemer's throat, trying to make the cub vomit, but it was of no use.

"We got to get you back to camp, if that antifreeze you lapped up isn't environmentally safe to animals, you are going to get awful sick in the next while. Goddamn it any way." There wasn't much else he could do other than keep his eye on the cub and watch for any signs of him getting sick. He had no idea how long it would take the poison to take effect. All he knew was that *antifreeze* killed.

"Come on lets head back to camp. We have to get as close to it as we can. Not sure how long before you'll start to get sick, if indeed that crap spewed all over the place isn't one of the animal friendly antifreeze products. There is no way I can know that. I'd rather be closer to camp in case you get sick." He poured what was left of the water in his canteen over the green stain in the snow, diluting it and perhaps making it less lethal. Then he and Redeemer descended into the forest.

A few hours later, he was relieved that Redeemer was showing no signs of poisoning. "You still feeling all right?" he candidly asked, as the cub bound toward him, rising on his hind legs in a playful gesture. Squatting he scratched the cub's belly. "It's getting late and we'll need to set up camp soon. I'm guessing if we walk another mile before dusk, we'll be close to camp. Not only that, but we'll be down low enough that we'll be able to set up for the night on grass. Rather than setting up in this snow, it'll be a lot more pleasant." Rising to his feet, the two companions descended once more into the undergrowth.

As predicted, an hour later they exited the cold forest. Finding a clearing where the ground was dry and green with grass, they set up for the evening. Bryce was relieved to be out of the snow. "Sure glad we've made it, it'll be warmer than up there," he pointed up the slope then added the last few cedar boughs to the roof of his lean-to. "There. That'll do for tonight. What do you think, does it look cosy enough?" Picking up his pack, he set it inside. Redeemer lay a short distance away, frolicking in the tall grass. He was content.

As the stars began to flicker in the darkening sky, and the flames from the fire danced gently on the warm evening breeze, Bryce curled up inside with the cub at his feet. *Sure glad he seems to be doing all right. I don't know what I would've been able to do had he got sick. Knock on wood,* thought Bryce as he closed his eyes.

Chapter 11

May 1, rising with the sun, Bryce crawled out of the lean-to and stretched. The cub still lay inside curled up in a ball. The fire from that past evening still smouldered, adding a few sticks he brought it back to life, and warmed up his hands. *What a beautiful morning,* he thought as he deeply inhaled the fresh scent of an early spring morning.

By now Redeemer was beginning to stir. He too yawned, stretching as he exited the shelter. "Good morning. How are you feeling today? You're looking good." Redeemer came to where Bryce sat, gently pawing at his shoulder. "Food, right?" He pulled a bag of beef jerky from his pack. "All we got for today is this jerky. We should be back at camp by noon. Then we'll have a real shindig of a meal, right from Bryce's kitchen." He handed the cub a handful of the jerked meat.

Bryce smiled as he looked on. *Yeah, I think he's going to be okay. He'd be sick by now if that crap he licked up yesterday was poisonous.*

Before noon that day, the two companions made their way back to their camp, no worse for wear, except a little tired and somewhat hungry. Still, camp never looked so good. "Well, here we are. Home sweet home." Bryce tossed his pack onto the table and sat down. "It's good to see nothing dramatic took place while we were gone. The tent is unruffled and the food cache looked all right when we passed it." There was a short pause while the two got comfortable. "You know what, I just realised it's the first of May. More of your bear relatives ought to be showing up soon. That's when things will get interesting. So far, things have been humdrum, at least from my perspective. If it weren't for you, Redeemer, I'd have been bored by now." He untied the knee-high moccasins and removed them, looking at his beat up shins.

The moccasins were certainly a treat to wear rather then the heavy boots he was used to, only thing was, they didn't protect the legs, and he was paying for that now. *Guess I best order in some boots after all. That reminds me I should take stock of what I need and don't need. I'm sure Jackson has forgot, although it was only a week ago when I spoke with him,* he looked out across the mirrored surface of Leroy Lake.

Towards the north-west, Rayne-Bow Foxeagle and her horse were coursing their way to Leroy Lake and Bryce's camp. Her purpose that day when she'd started, was clear. However, now that she had time to think it over, she wasn't sure a protest in Ottawa was such a good idea. Protests and such were done the first time Robertar & Robertar had wanted to develop the area sixteen years earlier. It helped put a stop to it then, but she knew also that back then there were a lot more people who opposed the idea, than there were today. *Strange how people, things, and ideas change,* Rayne reminisced. *I suppose change is good to a degree, but when change jeopardises livingthings it should not be allowed, or even considered.* "Nope. I'm going for it. We might not change the outcome, but we will certainly be heard. Giddy-up Gravy Train," Rayne said aloud as she heeled her horse.

Redeemer alerted Bryce to the oncoming horse and rider. He stood on his hind legs and sniffed the air with excitement, staring in the one direction. Bryce followed the bear cub's gaze and in a few moments caught sight of Rayne. "I'll be, if it isn't the enchantress of Toby Creek," he said as he stood from the table to go and meet his visitor. As always, Rayne was a sight of sheer beauty. "Hey, Rayne, I wasn't expecting you for a while. I was going to stop over in the next couple of days. Don't tell me you're having trouble with old Hector." He took the horse's reins.

"Nope. No trouble with Grandfather. In fact, he and I had a long talk yesterday. I've convinced him not to go to Ottawa," Rayne began.

"That is good news. To be honest I'm not sure what effect he'd have on the outcome."

"That's not all. We decided a group effort is more plausible, than if he were to go alone. That is why we're rallying all our elders, family and friends. All those who wish to join us are going to go Ottawa," she responded as she swung off her horse.

"What are you saying? A full-fledged protest or a quiet demonstration?" he asked with apprehension. He knew how ugly and violent a demonstration could turn.

"Do I hear a bit of concern?"

"Naturally, I've seen this type of thing before, was likely involved in a few *'things'* as well. It can turn ugly real quick. Nine out of ten times, it does nothing at all except make people angry. Are you sure you want to do something like that?"

"Definitely. Why wouldn't we?" she questioned as the two made their way to the table.

"No reason, really. You have to be organised and prepared for the worst. I've had buddies get beat up bad during and after such events. I imagine the cops in Ottawa can and will be as rough as the law will allow, if things get out of hand. I'm not trying to stop you from demonstrating, because that's a God given right. I only want you to be aware of what can happen."

"I'm glad you're not trying to stop us, 'cause the reason I'm here is because we were hoping you and any or all of your friends, and anyone else you can come up with, will join us."

A smile crossed his face as he stroked at his chin with contemplation. Back in his day, he was a master of protests. It had been ten years or more since he last protested anything, "How soon is all this coming together?"

"It's not going to happen overnight. After all, we do know the risks and we want to be as polite as possible. At first I wanted to leave everything up to the powers that be, but after contemplating and speaking with Grandfather further, I decided that our voices ought to be heard. Rest assured, Bryce, we're not going to rush the parliament building," she said with humor. "I'm hoping for early summer, perhaps the first part of June. It'll take at least that long to get organised and arrange transportation. What do you say? Are you in?"

"I am flattered that you'd ask. Only thing is, I'm not sure how far along with my research here I'll have gotten by then. I can't walk away from the work I'm doing, no matter how compelling a protest sounds. I'll certainly give it thought and will do whatever I can to help organise the onslaught, though I can't make any promises that I can attend. I know a slew of folks who live for this kind of thing." An old friend of his and Hector's, named Hayden, was one of the folks that came to his mind as he contemplated. Hayden owned and operated a hunting outfit. He was also an advocate in keeping the wild-lands, wild. "They'd likely jump on the bandwagon...oops I didn't mean that the way it might have sounded."

Rayne laughed at Bryce's apology. "No harm no foul. I knew what you meant. I do wish though that you would stand with us when the time comes. It would mean so much to Grandfather."

"Hey, come on; that isn't fair." He knew exactly what she was trying to do.

"It is true," responded Rayne with sincerity. "He'd be so happy to stand next to you in a fight as deep as this. I won't push the issue with you any longer though. I do understand that your work here is very important to the cause, the same cause we're going to protest in June. With that said, let's move on to conversation that is more pleasant. Like for instance, why are you in your stocking feet."

"Oh, that, well, Redeemer and I got back only a short while ago from an over-night jaunt, and my shins are somewhat banged up. I took the moccasins off to have a look and haven't slipped them back on yet. They are comfortable and warm, I'll give them that, but how are you supposed to wear them without getting banged up shins?" He lifted his pant leg showing the dozen or so cuts and bruises he sported. The two of them broke out into a giddy laugh.

"I have to say, that is awful funny. You poor guy. Everyone knows that you need the sixty-dollar retail versions. They at least come with a thin shin guard insert, see," Rayne responded as she removed the thin piece of plastic. "What you have on your feet, Bryce Ellwood, are one hundred percent, Grandfather-made, camp moccasins. They aren't made for long distance hiking. Why do you think he always wears boots?" Rayne broke out into a quiet chuckle as she averted her eyes toward Redeemer.

Bryce was dumbfounded for a few moments as he put the joke together. "What, you mean these *moccasins aren't made for walking.*" He sang out to the country tune of t*hese boots are made for walking.*

"Precisely," chortled Rayne.

"You've got to be kidding. Hector knew exactly what he was doing, didn't he. Pulled the wool over my eyes again, he did. I guess this relates back to what he always says, 'if you haven't walked a mile in an Indian's moccasins, you haven't walked a mile'." The two of them once more broke out into laughter, intensified now by the antics of Redeemer, who was playfully trying to frighten Rayne's horse. As fierce as he tried to portray himself, the red dun horse looked on at the cub as though he was completely bored. He darted toward Redeemer a time or two, until finally Redeemer relented and waddled back to the tent.

"The cub," Rayne started to break the silence that now enveloped them, "seems to be growing. You're looking good too. How have things been?" she questioned with admiration. Since the first time they met, Bryce had been in every one of her dreams. She admired everything about him, his work, his looks, and his humor. Even as shaggy looking as he was now, he was everything her heart desired, and she often wondered how he felt about her.

"Things have been good. Today they got better though…it's always nice to have a visitor stop by. It's even nicer when that visitor is you."

"Awe. That's sweet. Thank you."

"No need to thank me. It's the truth. Now tell me how things have been going for you and Hector. Good I hope?"

"Oh yes. I love visiting with Grandfather. He may be old but he never bores me. He has so much to teach, and I'm like a sponge for the wisdom he shares. Anyway, it's getting onto dusk and I still have to make my way back. By the way you never did tell me where you and Redeemer ventured to, that you had to spend the night outside."

"Right. I got side-tracked I guess. Yesterday there were some men up on the north-east ridge above the Ferlong Forestry road. We went to have a look. It was Robertar's men, likely hoping to do some early surveying. No work got done mind you, they had to pack her in 'cause they kept getting stuck. I found it rather comical, I mean really who in their right mind would attempt driving that road before June?" he half chuckled.

"No kidding, duh. Hard to believe that these are the men so many trust to develop this land. Senseless, isn't it?" Rayne stood and gathered her horse's reins.

"Indeed." he responded. "Are you sure that you have to head back."

"This time, yes. Besides, it is your turn to sleep over at my place, or should I say Grandfather's place. Trust me he won't mind." Rayne swung up onto her horse, blew Bryce a kiss, and set off for Toby Creek.

"I'll see you next week." he called after her. "Early next week that is. Be expecting me."

"We will, we will. See you then," came her reply as she crested the hill leading to the forest trail and home. The darkness of evening crept in fast, or so it seemed. He was weary and turned in before the silvery moon made its appearance. Tomorrow he would catch up again on his paperwork, and last but not least, he'd contact Jackson and order his supplies. Pulling the sheets from the cot over his shoulders, he closed his eyes.

Chapter 12

Dawn brought with it a light rain. The pitter-patter on the tent canvas is what woke Bryce. Yawning he sat up on the cot and slipped into his Levi jeans. His mission today was to catch up on paper work. He was glad it was raining. If it were sunny, in all likelihood the work he needed to catch up on, would go undone until tomorrow, and he knew tomorrow never came.

Redeemer was still curled up sound asleep. "Hey, rise and shine. I'll get some food cooking for us. Come on, get up." The cub rolled over and looked up toward Bryce, his eyes placid. "Well. Come on. Rise and shine little buddy." Bryce knelt beside him and he playfully rubbed Redeemer's belly. The cub finally rolled back over, stood, yawned, and stretched then followed him outside.

Looking to the north-west, Bryce took note of the black clouds billowing in, and it was evident they were in for a nasty storm. Redeemer could care little about the storm as he sat there waiting for his feeding. "I guess you're more interested in some eats, eh? Not to worry, I'm on it." Bryce turned on the camp stove.

With their stomachs full and before the storm hit, he did a quick walk around of the tent making sure it was secured enough to withstand the wind that was beginning to howl. He made his way inside, closing the tent's flap as the first wave of rain pelted down with anger. For three gruelling hours, the rain beat upon the tent like one playing a snare drum. Not wanting to risk any electronic equipment failures, he sat the rain out and instead continued with his paper work the old fashioned way, with a pen. As the rain subsided, he took a moment to step outside. The sun was now visible, ominously peeking out from the dark grey clouds, letting only a few rays shine down, it was a unique visual and he wasted no time in photographing the lustrous scene.

In moments, the dark clouds again obscured the rays of sun, and thunder broke out in the distance. Redeemer, frightened by the loud clap, darted inside and huddled at the tent entrance. Standing beneath the tent awning, Bryce waited patiently for the first flashes of lightning to compliment the photos he took. In the distance sheets of white-hot skidded across the dark impenetrable sky like camera flashes, followed by streaks of yellow threaded this way and that. "Wow. Now that was cool." he commented to himself, as he continued taking photos of the incredible sight. *Like sunsets, no two storms are ever alike,* he thought.

The spectacle over, except for the rain, Bryce retreated indoors. Taking up his pen and paper, he continued his work. For another hour and half as the rain relentlessly continued, he finished what he could of the writing he was behind on. He catalogued and dated the last paper folder he had in front. Closing it, he added it to the pile of others. Realising the time to be 2:00 p.m., he reached for his cell phone, dialling Jackson's number. With luck, he'd get through in a couple of tries. With the weather being as it was; he knew the signal would be weak. After a second attempt, Jackson picked up the phone on his end. "Hello, Conrad Jackson here," came the voice from the other end.

"Hey Jackson, how am I coming through on your end?"

"Bryce, is that you?"

"Sure is. I guess you can hear me eh? You're coming through as clear as day."

"Yep, I can hear you. Are you calling in your supply list?"

"That's right. I figured I best give you a reminder. Got a pen handy?"

"Give me a minute while I grab one." There was silence on the other end for a few seconds. "All right, fire away." Bryce read the list off to him, making sure to mention also that he needed boots. "Got it. That is quite a list, but I'll make sure it all gets to you. What happened to your other boots?" Jackson curiously asked.

"To make a long story short, let's just say I left them outside one night and something got a hold of them. Luckily, Hector over at Toby Creek, do you remember him?"

"Sure do."

"He had a pair of moccasins handy. Otherwise, I'd be barefoot."

"I see," Jackson chuckled. "Hector was one of the key players who helped convince Robertar to cease with their fight in developing those mountains the last time in '88. I bet Hector is as brazen and determined now as he was then. It's different this time though. Not sure you've been keeping up to date on the progress of Robertar's battle or should I say progress? It isn't good. Leastwise not from our perspective. Apparently though, letters of discontent are still arriving in those offices of government that can put a halt to it. Letters, though, aren't going to win this second battle."

"I couldn't agree with you more. Data, research, and proof of the devastation that the development will create to the fauna and flora of the area, are of the utmost importance in winning this time. That goes without saying. Anyway, Jackson, you got the list, and I should be expecting it when?" he wanted to confirm.

"Today is May 2, I can have it to you by the eighth, the tenth at the latest, unless, of course, you are in dire need of it now?"

"No, no. That's fine, make sure that the fly-boy that flies it in, puts it all up near the tent if I'm not around. Other than that, I have to get back to my doings. I'll be expecting the supplies no later than the tenth. Thanks, Jackson. I'll talk to you soon."

"You bet. Good bye."

Bryce turned off the phone and stretched out his legs. Outside the rain was still peppering the tent although not nearly as badly. With his hands behind his head he absorbed the quieting drone of the pitter-patter as the rain beat down on the canvas tent. It was maddening and serene all at once. Feeling a chill he stood and retrieved his flannel shirt then for the third time that day, stepped outside. The rain was soft now, and the gentle drizzle kept the remainder of the afternoon cool and damp.

A heavy fog surrounded Leroy Lake like an Angel's

halo. The still dark clouds obscured the late afternoon sun, and he smiled as he deeply inhaled. He had always loved the scent left behind after a good downpour, and here at Leroy Lake the scent was even more dulcet. Turning on the camp stove, he called for Redeemer. At first, the cub was reluctant to step outside. The thunder that scared him earlier that day had made him less then receptive to Bryce's calling.

Sticking only his head outside, he sniffed at the air. "Hey, little buddy. What's the matter? Come on, come over; its safe," Bryce gently coaxed. "I'm whipping us up some chow. I have coffee going for me, a pot full of leftover this and that, for you. You're not still frightened by that thunder we heard earlier, are you?" he chuckled knowing it was indeed the case. After more coaxing Redeemer sauntered over to the table and with the big pot of food between his front paws, he lay down and fed. "See, not so scary after all, is it?" Bryce chortled, bringing the hot coffee he held in his hands, to his lips.

As the two sat in the company of one another, the dark menacing clouds slowly lifted and a sporadic pallid-blue sky appeared. "It's going to be a nice one tomorrow. We should head up to the beaver pond we spotted. I'm sure things might have changed since we were last there. The beaver kits if there are any, will likely be venturing outside their dens. We might get lucky and film a few." Turning his gaze toward Leroy Lake, he contemplated the idea. The only ripples the unstirred lake produced were brought on by the gentle sprinkle of rain. Everything was calm, fresh, and quiet.

By dusk the entire sky opened up, and a rainbow skirted across the lake. The fading sun came on hot. Before the first stars flickered that calm evening, the lightly saturated ground was no longer damp. The flora surrounding both his camp and Leroy Lake was as brilliant as always after a good wetting, and the vivid colours screamed with pleasure. *There is nothing like a good downpour to make the flora smile like that,* he reminisced. Three hours later and exhausted from a day of writing and gloomy weather, he turned in.

Chapter 13

They got an early start that morning, as they hiked up to the beaver dams they'd discovered days earlier on Jack Pine Creek. The creek, although deep and cold, was not as ferocious as it had been, and on occasion the cub took it upon himself to wade into the cool water as the late morning sun beat down on them. "Sure a beautiful day isn't it?" Bryce questioned the bear cub.

Redeemer couldn't agree more as he bound toward him, rubbing his wet head against his legs. Smiling, Bryce scratched Redeemer behind the ear. "Only a mile or so to go, little buddy then we'll finally be able to rest. I imagine the beaver will be out in full-force today, with it being as hot as it is. Quite warm now I'd say, and it's only 11 o'clock. Come on, let's make tracks." Turning, they continued north-east along the creek.

Redeemer darted past and headed the jaunt; he knew exactly where they were going. "For being a little fellow and only being here once before, you sure seem to know where you're going. That's good, I'm glad." For a moment in time, Bryce lost himself in admiration of the area as he looked around. It was distressing and inordinate that people, not all people, but a good majority, would rather see a ski resort carved into the mountains than the beauty of the mountains themselves. He couldn't understand why people were bent on displacing the land and the things that flourished there. The only answers he knew were commerce, power, and control. "The three evils," he softly muttered. Shaking his head, he continued onward.

Breaking through the brush less than an hour later, they finally made the distance to the beaver dams. The dam itself had doubled in size, and the body of water was as clear as glass, not a ripple lapped at the grassy shore. "Look at that, the beaver have been busy I'd say." He looked across the pond, noting how the area where they sat the last time, was now flooded. "Well, we won't be sitting there," he said as he pointed his chin. Finding an area that was both dry and protected by a big cedar, he leaned his .308 against an old log, removing his shoulder pack containing his cameras and gear.

"Ah, that's better," he started as he stretched his back and shoulders, relieving the strain the gear caused. "As soon as I have these cameras set up the way I want, we'll have a snack," he said as he looked over to where Redeemer lay in big patch of mountain clover. "Hey, great pose. Hold on a second, I have to have a picture of that." Fidgeting with his digital camera, he tried to get the best photo of the young cub as it lay there, lulled by the peace that could only be found in such a place.

Like a professional model, Redeemer took it upon himself to strike different poses, and Bryce captured them all. "You're a big ham, you know that?" he commented as he smiled. It took a few extra minutes to set up his tripod and 35mm camera. Finally satisfied with both the camera angle and view, he stepped back. "You know, I might be convinced to walk up past these dams. I'd like to see what's up that way. First though, let's have a snack." Squatting, he reached into his pack to retrieve a bag of jerky and some dried bananas, which they shared over the course of a few minutes.

"Well, that's that. How are you feeling? Feel like leading a jaunt upstream some, maybe a half mile or so?" he questioned himself as well as Redeemer.

Redeemer seemed quite content to loll in the sun and he didn't respond except with a yawn and stretch. "All right. You can hang here if you like. I'm going to take a jaunt upstream. Whenever you feel the need to join me, feel free." The pond was ominously quiet as he coursed his way along its shore. The stillness seemed eerie, yet placid. He packed with him only the rifle, digital camera and his daypack, which held minimal supplies.

Every step he took in the undergrowth or on the grassy shore, echoed with clarity. Every crunch of his footstep, every slosh his moccasins made on the mud soaked creek shore as he coursed his way north, came to life. He stopped frequently to both listen to the silence and to admire the virgin forest he was in. Things, he knew, had a way of changing in terrain as deep and wild, knowing this he remained cautious and alert as he continued.

In the distance he could hear the sound of a waterfall, and decided it would be at that point of the creek where he'd turn back. The distance to the waterfall seemed no less than a few hundred yards from where he now stood, however, getting to it could prove interesting. First, he had to hike up and over a rocky precipice scattered thick with patches of stinging nettle. The top was a forest darkened by mammoth fir and spruce, and scattering the rocky forest floor was years and years of rotting deadfall covered in moss. The large pines stood tall and were cloaked thickly with branches, letting little sunlight through, and the ground remained damp from the days past rainfall. Indeed, it would be a slippery jaunt for one wearing moccasin's.

He shrugged his shoulders; *I can't imagine it's much further.* Repositioning the .308 rifle that hung over his shoulder, checking the daypack and tightening the belt around his waist that kept the pack secure then he stepped forward, beginning to course his way across the top of the rocky precipice. Stopping occasionally, he took photos of the flora, and fungi that grew on the organically sufficient forest floor. It reminded him of Alice in Wonderland, and he chuckled. *Glad I came up this way. Quite an impressive little ecosystem carrying on as though nothing mattered. Impressive, indeed.* Turning he worked his way over to the edge of the precipice and looked down. From where he stood, he guessed the distance to the rocky shore below to be at least a hundred feet straight down.

Looking out across the narrow gorge to the other side of the creek, he noted how the forest on that side gently sloped to the creek edge. It was as dark and as thick as the one he was in now. Above it all, and looking down, he felt like a king. The waterfall, he knew, was only a short distance away; he could hear the loud thundering as he approached closer. Finally stepping out of the thick brush, he stepped onto the rocky shore above the roaring falls.

Camera in hand, he began taking photos. At last

finding his way to a rocky outcrop that overlooked the falls, he sat down. He was completely awe-struck at the sheer beauty. The afternoon sun shone on the wet outcropping of rock that the falls shot over, making them glisten, and a rainbow near the bottom was as permanent as the big rock he sat on. He took note that the distance across to the other side was less than sixty feet, and he could tell it would be easy enough to cross, even if he had to wade into the water upstream a bit.

Whatever it would take, he wanted to get to the far side so he could climb down to the bottom of the falls. He'd hike the creek back to his camera and gear on the opposite side is all. He was somewhat disappointed that Redeemer hadn't joined him, but the cub had made his choice back at the dams. Besides, there were too many dangers up this way, and it would have been difficult for him to watch out not only for himself, but also for the cub.

Rested he stood and began to wade across the cold creek. He had taken only a few steps when he lost his footing. Fighting to prevent himself from being swept over the falls, he let go of the rifle as the cold water rushed him, and like a log, he was tossed over.

Coming to sometime later, he found himself at the bottom of the waterfall, lying on the rocky creek shore. His body and face ached with pain as he sat up, trying to stand to no avail. His clothes were blood-soaked from the gashes he'd sustained from the fall. The wounds still bled and his left leg was crippled; he could not move it. Raising his hand to his forehead, he felt the first gouging lesion, a cut he knew that was in dire need of stitching. Out there, though, there were no doctors, out there... he was alone.

He lay back down as dizzy spells of pain overtook him, lying motionless as everything spun. Clenching his teeth, he sat up in agony, reaching out to his left leg. The swelling confirmed that it was broken. Blood trickled into his eyes as he banged his fists into the ground. Lying down once more in great pain, he looked up to the sky, blood from the wounds on his face and forehead now dribbled into his ears. "God damn it," he murmured still clenching his teeth. Then darkness overcame him, as pain scudded through his body, prompting him to pass out.

The buzzing flies around his face and ears woke him, and for a moment he wondered what happened. Then it all became clear once more as the painful sensation of his broken leg and the cuts to his face, head, and back, erupted in searing agony. Inhaling deeply and squinting in pain, he brushed at the flies feeding on the dried blood covering his face. Sitting up, he looked at his leg, grateful that he hadn't sustained a compound fracture. Still though, the pain was unbearable, and he knew the only way he would be able to remedy the break and unendurable pain, was to set the broken bone himself. Looking around for something he could use to help with the task, he spotted two large rocks partially buried, *perfect,* he thought. Crawling, he inched his way toward them. He would have to put his leg between them and with all the strength he could muster, reef it using the rocks to pry it back to its normal position. He knew it wouldn't be a very clean fix, but he had no other choice if he wanted to make it out of the bush alive.

Making the distance, he grimaced in pain as he positioned his leg. Taking a deep breath he counted to three then with the anger of a madman pried his leg between the two rocks. The audible sound of the broken bone as it snapped back into place, echoed in the forest, as did his squeals of agony. Reeling in pain, he passed out. Hours passed until finally a hoot from an owl disrupted his slumber, and he woke to a darkening evening.

Shivering in agony, he sat up, his back to one of the rocks. A few paces away on the rocky shore he spotted his rifle and his spirits rose. Taking a few deep breaths, he cringed; standing then hobbling to the rifle, he retrieved it. He had a lifeline now.

Grasping the rifle barrel with his hand, he used it as a walking stick as he limped his way back to the rocks then sitting down heavily, he sighed. *It's going to be a rough go until I can make it back to camp. Likely, it's going to take me a few days. Hope, Redeemer finds his way back. I wish he joined me.* The wounds to his face and forehead stopped bleeding, yet the pain remained as constant as the throbbing of his leg. What he needed was a splint. Looking toward the darkening woods, he winced in pain as he rose, coursing his way to a large aspen, he broke off two of the thickest branches that were within his reach, making sure they were long enough that he'd be able to cut them into four pieces. *These will have to do,* he thought as he hobbled back to the rocks, the branches in his hand.

Sitting, he removed his buck knife, gently cutting off his pant leg below his knee. With the same dexterity he cut the two branches in half. The first two pieces he placed on either side of his leg, using strips from his pant leg and leather from his moccasins, which he cut off above his ankle, securing the thick limbs to his leg. The last two he placed on his calf and shin, and as firmly as the others he tied those as well. The pain was excruciating, but he fought it off. With the task done, he rested waiting for the pain he caused his leg, to subside. After what seemed like eternity, the throbbing agony dissipated, and he was able to doze.

He'd been out for only a short while, when he felt a wet nose brush against his cheek and a tongue lick his face. Startled to wakefulness, he was relieved to see Redeemer. "How did you find me?" he started in a listless voice, " I'm sure glad you did." The cub gently pawed at him, knowing he'd been hurt. "Yeah, I'm in a bit of a mess. I took a tumble over the falls. I'm a lot better now that you're here." He looked into cub's eyes. "We're going to have to stay here tonight. Make yourself comfortable. We'll try to make some distance tomorrow, but until then I need rest."

Chapter 14

The following morning, after a night of fitful sleep with no shelter to protect them from the cold, and by the light of day, he was able to have a better look at his leg. The deep black and purple bruising looked as though someone used a sledgehammer to smash it. It felt that way too, and he grimaced. Taking a deep breath, he slowly rose, still using the rifle as a walking stick; he hobbled to the creek shore to quench his thirst and to throw water onto his face. The glacial water felt good on the wounds he endured as he washed away the dried blood from his face and forehead.

The lesions, as painful as they were, no longer concerned him. The pain from his leg was a different story though, and it made him feel sick to his stomach. Looking up to the waterfall, he shook his head. It was a wonder he hadn't been killed. The jagged rocks jutting out were menacing enough to have easily taken his life, and he realised how lucky he was.

A few paces from where he stood, Redeemer was thirstily lapping at the water. There was a school of pocket-sized trout that flashed from out of nowhere, which caught his eye, and he jumped in after the small fish. Bryce was able to let a smile cross his face as he watched Redeemer's antics. "Hey, little fella, I don't think those fish are overly keen on letting you snack on them." Finally giving up the chase, the cub sloshed out of the cool water and shook himself spattering Bryce. "Couldn't you have done that elsewhere?" he questioned as he slowly turned and hobbled back to the rocks where they'd spent the night.

Sitting down with his left leg outstretched, he winced in pain. "I'm going to have to find a good walking stick. I don't want to be bent over like an old man using this rifle as a cane. I don't imagine we'd be able to make much distance that way. What I need is a nice thick 'Y' shaped stick I can use as a crutch. Have you seen anything like that, Redeemer?" he asked as though the bear cub understood. Redeemer gently sniffed at his leg and face then drew his coarse tongue across it.

"Yeah, yeah. We'll get moving in a few minutes. That little jaunt to the creek caused me a great deal of hurt; my leg throbs like you wouldn't believe. Give me a minute." Sighing, he slowly rose. "All right, let's head downstream." he said as he finally stood, using the rifle as a cane. "First thing we got to do is find a good walking stick or crutch. I imagine we'll find one over yonder." He gestured with his chin in the direction of a stand of a big fir a few paces away. It took a few minutes for him to make the distance, but when he finally did, he found what he was looking for. "Yep, this one will work." He hacked at the branch with his knife until the thick branch let loose from the tree. Testing it, he made sure it would hold his weight. "Looks like I've found what I've been looking for. Are you ready to make some tracks?" Inhaling deeply he shouldered the rifle.

They coursed their way for two miles along the shore before he finally had to rest. His leg throbbed worse than ever, and it caused him to sweat in agony. Looking onward in the direction they travelled, he could see that they'd have to head into the forest. The rocky creek shore which lay ahead, was scattered with both large rocks and old logs and would undoubtedly cause him a great deal of inconvenience. The forest was his only hope, at least until they passed what lay ahead.

The creek echoed as it rumbled by. The cold water splashed at them as though a heavy downpour of rain was pelting them, but it felt good in the late morning sun. He looked down to Redeemer who was looking on at what lay ahead as curiously as he had. "No, we're not going to hike along that mess. We'll head into the bush over there," he pointed at a game trail he happened to gaze upon in the few minutes they'd rested. It was obviously the best route to take. The last thing he wanted to do was to break his other leg trying to save them time. He winced then nodded, as he set foot toward the game trail.

The trees grew tall and thick, reaching up to the sky like skyscrapers. Rays from the late morning sun streaked into the woods here and there. It was a beautiful sight, which under normal conditions he would have photographed, even if in pain. However that wouldn't be the case, he lost his daypack and digital camera when he took the spill over the waterfall, all he had was his knife and the rifle. That in itself was a Godsend. Resting a few short minutes, he looked at the unmingled beauty that was canopied beneath the big evergreens. Then sighing, he grimaced as he repositioned the rifle on his shoulder and continued onward.

Following the game trail easterly until the sound of the creek was distant, they cut south and continued until again the sound of rushing water was close by. Finally breaking out of the forest they were again on the rocky shore, a good mile and half downstream. It was as far as the pain was willing to let him travel that day, a total of three, maybe four miles. Now he ached for a place to rest.

Looking along the shore, he spotted an alcove, and he made for it. It was close to the creek, and with luck, Redeemer might have a chance at getting himself a fish. Bryce on the other hand wanted only rest, though his stomach growled with hunger as he looked around. He cringed as he sat, making himself comfortable. "You know what I'd really like, Redeemer? I'd like to find my daypack along the shore." he commented as he stretched out his broken leg. In it, he knew was enough stuff to keep him going, until he made it back to camp. Inhaling deeply he looked toward Redeemer. "Ah, we'll be okay. Isn't that right?" he waved his hand through the air as though he was swatting at a fly as he assured himself.

The mid-afternoon soon slipped away to early evening, and a chill was in the air. "We might as well burrow in for the evening. I think we're in for another cool evening." He adjusted his leg, making himself comfortable, only to be interrupted by a rustle in the woods behind him. Redeemer too, heard the sound and darted to Bryce's side. Reaching for his rifle, he cocked it. He turned his head, but he saw nothing. Redeemer rose on his hind legs and stood vigilant. Whatever had been in the bushes was now gone, and silence enveloped the two companions.

"I guess you scared off what might have been an intruder. Good for you, you're a brave little cub. It's okay now."

The following morning as they coursed their way again along the creek, he took notice that the water was not moving as quickly as it was a few miles upstream, however it was still too swift for him to attempt crossing. Resting for a few minutes, he adjusted the splint on his leg. The pain caused him to grit his teeth as he made the final adjustment. Satisfied he took a deep breath, shouldering the rifle before the two set afoot. Coming around a bend in the creek, Bryce caught glimpse of something blue. He wasn't sure but it looked like his daypack. Stopping, he squinted at the object that was precariously hooked on an old tree that jutted out of the bank on the other side and partially immersed in the creek. Sure enough, it was his daypack. "Look, there it is. There's my daypack," he said with enthusiasm as he pointed at it.

Regrettably, there was no way he could get to it. The water was well over his head in depth, and it rushed by like a concord at that particular spot. There was no way he could even wade out to get it, in his condition. The only thing he could do was try to shoot the branch off. If he was lucky enough, the daypack might then float to the surface, and wash up on shore a few yards away.

Removing the rifle from his shoulder, he took aim at the old tree branch. The shot echoed in the still morning; the reverberation from the big .308 caused shock waves of agony to shoot down his broken leg, and he dropped the rifle. Looking at the branch with watery eyes, he was disappointed that his shot wasn't true, and that the blue pack remained hanging on to the old branch deep beneath the water. *Damn, five more shots left. This time I'm going to sit.*

He lowered his body to the ground with his left leg straight out in front of him. Picking up the .308, he brought it up to his shoulder, sighting in on the branch. It was the first time in his life that he was leery in firing a rifle. His mind raced with the pain he experienced not five minutes earlier. Inhaling deeply, he oxygenating his blood then slowly squeezed the trigger. The blue pack bubbled up to the surface and jetted across the water, topsy-turvy as it went. *Nice shooting Tex,* he smiled as he slowly rose.

Redeemer caught sight of the daypack as it floated closely to the creek shore. Curiosity or plain common sense, caused the cub to wade into the water, clasp the object in his jowls, and wade back to shore. Bryce watched in disbelief as he hobbled the distance to where Redeemer now had the pack between his front paws, and was ruthlessly sniffing at it.

His mouth salivated as he finally got the pack away from Redeemer and opened it. The contents inside, because of the waterproof pack, remained as dry as the day he put them in there. The smell from the beef jerky wafted up to his nostrils as he feverishly pulled the bag out. Tossing a piece to Redeemer, he stuffed a piece into his own mouth. "That is some good eats." He reached for another, his mouth still full from the first, swallowing he gobbled the second piece just as quickly. Minutes turned into hours as they rested, and soon the western sky turned crimson.

Staring at the sunset, his mind raced with how lucky he'd actually been. *Thing's could've been a lot worse. Might not have found that daypack. That and the rifle are our lifelines now,* he reminisced as he gazed on.

Redeemer came over and lay down at his side, curling up into a ball he yawned then closed his eyes. For a few minutes, they both sat in silence. Finally Bryce slowly rose to gather firewood. A task he knew would be difficult in his condition. Nonetheless a task needed doing regardless of circumstances, tonight he wanted a fire and tonight he would have one.

It took close to an hour to gather enough deadfall and driftwood, but finally the task was done. Sighing in relief, he settled for the evening. The fire lifted his spirit and a calm came over him as he looked deep into the orange flames. The heat was as welcoming as the sound the wood made as it snapped and crackled, shooting sparks into the darkening sky like fireflies dancing on a gentle breeze. He added more wood, and the warmth from the flames lulled him to sleep.

Chapter 15

The fire from the night before, continued to glow in the early morning twilight. Adding a stick, he waited for the flames to come to life then he warmed his hands above the flame. He'd slept well, considering all things and how his leg awakened him from time to time with dizzying pain. His exhaustion though, helped get him some sleep, and he wrestled with the pain all night. Now as he sat there in the dim light of day, he looked over his broken leg. To all accounts, in his opinion, it appeared to be healing. It would remain black and blue for weeks to come, that was a given. He could see no reason why the pain had been so aggressive during the night, and he shrugged his shoulders. *Part of the healing process I guess,* he thought, adding another stick to the flames.

Redeemer began to stir, and he looked over to Bryce with weary eyes. "Good morning. How did you sleep last night? I had a bit of a fight, what with all the pain my leg insisted I be in. It doesn't feel so bad now. In fact, it feels somewhat better than it did yesterday, or for that matter last night. We'll be able to put some miles behind us today." Reaching into his daypack, he retrieved some jerky, tossing a thick slap to Redeemer then took one for himself. "We'll let this fire die out before we start off. It won't be much longer. It's pretty much beginning to peter out now," he said as he chewed on the jerky.

As the coals turned to ash and the last flame fluttered, he rose, and using the butt of his rifle, he turned dirt over into the smouldering coals. "There, that'll take care of that. Are you ready to move? Come on, let's make tracks." Adjusting the rifle around one shoulder and tucking the crutch under the other, they set off. They made good progress and by mid-day the beaver dams came into view. "There it is," he smiled and sighed as he looked on. "Not much further. Let's get." he said while they drew closer. They were on the opposite side, but crossing the calm water wouldn't be an impossible task; difficult yes, impossible no.

Making the distance, he cringed as he sat down on the

grassy shore to rest. From where he sat, he could faintly make out the camera and spare gear he had left behind on the other side. He was relieved, to say the least, that it all appeared to be intact. The two problems he faced, were how he was going to cross the calm waters, and how he was going to pack all the gear with his bum leg. Obviously he'd have no choice but to leave some stuff. He could always retrieve it later. That took care of problem two.

How he would cross to the other side without too much difficulty was yet to be figured. Walking along the dam that stretched from one side to the other was out of the question, and trying to swim was a no go. There was no way he'd be able to handle the pain. The water he knew was easily over his head, so wading across was out of the question as well. He could perhaps hike downstream, maybe find a narrow crossing that was neither deep nor swift then hike back up on the side he needed to be on, something he wasn't willing to do. Instead, he sat in contemplation, looking around for any means to get him to the other side.

He noticed a fair-sized log stuck in the dam close enough to the shore that he might be able to untangle it from the branches, poles, and mud the beavers plastered it with. It was big enough he assumed, that he could use it to float across. The work in untangling it though, would likely cause him a great deal of pain. He contemplated the idea, concluding it was the only one he had. Holding his gaze of the log, he heard a smack of a beaver's tail slap at the water, warning the others of their presence. He was able to catch a glimpse of the large beaver as it splashed then dove beneath the calm water, sending ripples that caressed the shore. *Huh, that was neat,* he thought as he looked on.

Redeemer also took an interest, swimming out to where the beaver had been, only to be discouraged that the odd animal was no longer there. He swam in circles a few times, turned and swam back to shore. There was a glint of both apprehension and confusion across his face as he made land, and darted to Bryce's side. "Yeah, I know, beavers are peculiar. Likely, it's the first one you've seen. Not to worry;

there's nothing to fear of them. They belong here as all the other animals do, including you and me," he explained; as the bear cub shook himself dry.

Averting his gaze once more on the task of removing the log from the dam, he scratched the top of his head, trying to visualise how to proceed, but no matter how hard he tried to visualise, he knew there was no easy or painless way to tackle the task. He'd simply have to grin and bear it. Giving his head a shake he slowly rose, grimacing in pain as he did. Finally standing upright, he hobbled without his crutch the distance to the dam. Each pace he took caused him to wince and grit his teeth. The pain was so brutal it caused his eyes to water, and tears streamed down his dirty unshaven face.

Making the distance, he stood on his one good leg and inhaled deeply, concentrating his efforts on letting go of the agonising pain he'd subjected himself to. Minutes passed before the pain subsided to where he was comfortable enough to proceed. Stepping into the cold water he waded up to his knees, dragging his bum leg along the muddy bottom, and balancing himself with the other. The cold water was a welcome relief, and he stood still as the soothing waters caressed his damaged leg. Then, he began the process of removing the log he hoped would support him when he swam to the other side.

It wasn't long before the cub joined in. He too pulled, tugging effortlessly at the poles and such that mired the log. He really had no idea what Bryce was attempting, but it certainly looked fun. "That a boy. Keep it up little buddy and we'll get this painful task done in no time." They worked at it for close to an hour then finally, with one last tug, the log broke away from the dam and surfaced. It floated like an anchored boat waiting to set sail, and Bryce smiled. "We did it, we finally have a way to cross, or at least I do. You on the other hand can swim the distance. Come on let's head back to shore. We'll cross to the other side once I've rested a bit." Turning he slowly guided the log to shore, Redeemer paddling close behind.

Hobbling to the shoreline, he winced with pain as he

sat down, while the log bobbed and swayed this way and that. Redeemer pawed and wrestled with it until finally realising the log wasn't fighting back, and he soon lost interest. It was a beautiful spring day and the sun shone brightly on the calm water, which reflected the blue sky in its mirrored surface. Bryce took notice of the three beaver sitting on their dens, gawking and chatting at him with curiosity. It brought a smile to his face, and for a few moments he lost himself in the serenity of the present, even the pain he felt in his leg escaped him.

Redeemer, now aware of the odd creatures, stood on his hind legs, and gawked back. A low muffled growl followed, and he abruptly dashed into the water. The beaver however tucked and dove out of sight then were gone. This time the cub swam the distance to the beaver den and climbed on top. Bouncing up and down, he tried digging his way into the den, to no avail. Giving up, he lay down on top as though he were totally exhausted, gently pawing at the water. Eventually bored with that, he swam back to shore, and to Bryce's side.

"You'll never get to play with them if you keep scaring them." Bryce commented as Redeemer sat next to him. Reaching into his daypack, he retrieved the half-finished bag of jerked meat. Sharing a few pieces, they sat in silence as they gnawed, butterflies fluttered by and birds sang their songs, echoing through the silent woods. An overwhelming peace enveloped them both and with drowsy eyes, they lay down. The sun caressed Bryce's face like a mother's warm breath, all the pain he felt in his leg subsided, and in moments, he was fast asleep.

It was dusk when they finally awoke. To his astonishment and disappointment, the log had tactfully been fixed into the beaver dam once more. "Look at that, the beavers took possession of our log." he half-chuckled, and half stammered at the scenario he was now in. "Tonight we sleep here, I guess. We'll have to get that log back tomorrow. My leg isn't up to the task again today. Dumb luck or what? Should've anchored it better, or shouldn't have dosed off," he commented as he rubbed his chin in disbelief.

He would never have thought that they would've done that. Slowly rising and cringing in pain, he gathered some nearby wood, moments later bringing the flame to life. It was a small fire, but the heat emitting from the orange flames would keep him warm throughout the long night ahead.

As dusk turned to evening, he sat close to the flames, watching as they flickered, casting shadows across the calm water. It was serene, and their serenity was broken only when the woods behind them began to rustle. Redeemer rose on his hind legs, looking intently in the direction of the sound as he sniffed at the air.

Without warning, a mangy black bear dashed out from behind a stand of mountain ash, coursing its way toward them, stopping only short of the fire as it rose on its hind legs. Redeemer growled as fiercely as he could. The black bear answered back with a muffled snort, shaking its head from side to side. Bryce grabbed for the .308 and fired into the air.

The startled intruder turned tail and headed for higher ground. The sound of it crashing through the forest brought a sigh of relief to them both. "I've never seen a bear come that close to open flames before. I wouldn't have stood much of a chance if he decided to move toward me. Thanks to you we showed him," chuckling he tossed a few more sticks onto the fire to bring up the flames, and again, silence enveloped them, and the peace returned. Remaining cautious, he dozed with the rifle across his legs, his finger on the trigger and one eye open.

By 10:00 a.m. the following morning, they managed to remove the log from the dam and were sitting soaking wet on the far shore where he had left his camera and gear. The tripod, he knew, would have to be picked up later. It was too bulky and heavy for him to pack with his leg being as it were. Painstakingly, he removed the camera from the tripod, and put it in its case, covering the tripod with a sweater and a few boughs that he was able to pull from a cedar.

"We'll have a short break then head for home," he said as he shuffled through his backpack, checking on the food he'd left behind. He was surprised it had not been touched.

Retrieving a few power bars he opened them, and gave one to the cub. "That'll keep you going for a bit. We'll stop again downstream," he commented as he ate one of the bars himself. Finally rested and somewhat dry, they headed for Leroy Lake, the backpack securely placed around his shoulders and strapped at his waist.

They continued for close to a mile before his leg flashed with agonising strain as though it were on fire, and he cringed as he slowly sat. Inhaling deeply, he shook his head as he cautiously removed the pack. He knew then that there was no way they'd make the distance to camp before noon the next day.

Looking toward Redeemer, he wiped the sweat from his brow. "I need to rest for a bit. My leg's beginning to throb, and you look as though you could use a bite to eat." He reached for the food. "I could probably use some energy too. We have an unopened can of peanuts; that ought to put the poop back into us." he opened the can, and gave a big handful to Redeemer.

Whatever little amount of energy the peanuts gave to the cub was enough, and soon Redeemer was splashing about in the cool water. Bryce watched, sitting motionless. Every breath he took caused him to wince in dizzying pain. He couldn't tell if his leg was mending or not, he could only hope. Clenching his teeth, he tried wiggling his toes but couldn't. Pain shot through his body like flames from hell, making his eyes water. Shrinking back from the pain, he averted his eyes to Redeemer who was still frolicking in the water. Although in pain, a smile crossed his face.

Redeemer's character was audacious, nothing less. The cub showed little fear when coming face to face with potential foes. It was a trait bred into him, a trait that all animals were given in order to endure the wildness of their home. To be that close to something as wild as Redeemer was a dream come true, and from that he drew his strength.

Inhaling deeply a few more times, he waited for the throbbing pain in his leg to subside, his mind slowly going blank to the agony he was in. Finally rested, he stood. "Come on Redeemer, let's make tracks while the sun is still hot. I figure we can make another mile or two before we'll need to stop again." He adjusted both his packsack and rifle, leaning on the crutch, he slowly started off with Redeemer close behind. The hot sun mercilessly beat down on them as they walked. The smell of pine and cedar wafted in the gentle blowing breeze; which helped to keep them cool, and Bryce was thankful for that.

They coursed their way along the creek non-stop, until his leg throbbed with pain. He estimated that they were perhaps five maybe six miles from camp, a distance he knew he wouldn't be able to make. He decided he'd gone far enough. Tomorrow with luck and determination regardless of the pain, he'd make every effort to reach Leroy Lake.

Finding a level area beneath the low hanging branches of a cedar, he made camp. "We'll stay here tonight, Redeemer." He made himself comfortable. "The worst part of the hike is behind us now. Downstream a half a mile or so, the terrain gets easier. We'll make better progress then." He wanted to make that distance now, but he knew it was fruitless. The pain would only get worse if they continued.

There'd be no way he could stay at Leroy Lake with a broken leg, and be able to do all that needed doing. He needed treatment, that was a given. Perhaps he could get Rayne to carry on while his leg mended? *First things first,* he thought. *I have to make it back to camp and go from there.* The more he thought about it, the more determined he was to make it happen. It would give Rayne the practical experience she craved.

Adding a few more sticks to his fire, he patiently waited for the coffee to be done. It was the first he'd had in four days. It was the May 7. In three more days he was expecting the supplies he ordered, and with luck he'd be back at camp. Then, he would fly out to a hospital with whomever Jackson sent. It wouldn't give him much time to make arrangements with Rayne, and contacting her would be tough. In his state, the ten-mile hike to Toby Creek was out of the question. It was another bridge he'd have to cross, and he couldn't cross that bridge until he made it safely back to camp.

Back at the Kootenay forestry airstrip, Cameron Kane was looking over the list of supplies he was solicited to deliver to Bryce. Two days earlier, he turned down a $250,000.00 USD contract. With that kind of cash, he could have retired. Then he discovered his client was Roberto Robertar. They threw a few words back and forth, and a threat or two was made. Cameron had heard spew like that before and had thought nothing of it. He simply told Roberto to find another pilot 'to kiss his ass'. That was the end of it. Simple.

"Is all this stuff boxed and ready, Jackson? Or am I supposed to pack it?" Cam asked as he leaned forward in the leather chair across from Jackson's big desk.

"Nope, that's been taken care of. It'll be ready first thing tomorrow, which leads me to a question, where are you staying tonight?"

"I'm here now. Not going to fly out to Cranbrook then fly back this way tomorrow. I'll sleep in the Mantis tonight, if that's all right with you?"

"Sure, that works. It's going on to 8:00 p.m. now, I'm heading for home. Care to join the wife and me for dinner, Cam?"

"Thanks, but no thanks, I think I'll hang out here. I got some sandwiches and whatnot in the helicopter."

"All right." The two men rose and exited the ground level office onto the New Kootenay landing strip. "See you in the morning. Coffee's on at 6:00 a.m. Goodnight," said Jackson as he walked through the chain link gate.

"Yep. See you tomorrow." Cam waved as he walked the short distance to his helicopter 'The Yellow Mantis'. Getting comfortably inside, he grabbed his lunch cooler and thermos, flipped on the portable DVD player he kept in the helicopter, and sat back to watch the home DVD he'd documented of his flights into the backcountry. Some of the territory where he made deliveries, pickups, drops, etc, in the past were places that no other bush pilot would consider going. Cam though, knew his abilities and what he could and couldn't do. It was just that no other pilots were crazy enough to try. Besides, it was good for business.

It was because of his experience that Roberto Robertar wanted him for the contract in getting things underway in the Purgatorys. The five star ski resort, although still not passed by legislation, in Roberto Robertar's opinion was undoubtedly going to be *passed*. He wanted Cam to deliver supplies, land surveyors, and slashing crews to get things underway. When Cam denied, Roberto Robertar was at a loss in finding anyone with his qualifications, or any other pilot willing to give him the light of day.

To him, time was money, and money was time, neither of which he wanted to waste. Picking up the phone Roberto dialled Cam's cell number; he was going to offer Cam the contract one last time. The phone vibrated in Cam's pocket, and he reached for it. "Hello. Cam here."

"Hello, Cam, this is Roberto. Listen, we may have got off on the wrong foot." There was a pause as Roberto took a long drag from the cigar in his mouth.

"I don't think so. I'm not interested in being a vessel for you or anyone else you hire to destroy the Purgatorys. I told you that already."

"Listen. I'll offer you another fifty thousand dollars. I've already lost that amount in the past couple days with no work going on up there."

"Another fifty grand isn't going to change my mind; nor is another two hundred and fifty thousand. There's no amount you can offer me that will change my mind. Now if you don't mind, I'll tell you again. I'm not interested."

"Still isn't good enough for you eh? You're costing me more money than your small-scale flight agency makes in a year. I'll see to it that you eat dirt," Roberto bellowed as he hung up the phone.

"What a freak!" Cam said out loud as he turned off his cell, shaking his head in disgust. The DVD had ended by now and Cam removed it, shutting off the player, he reclined the seat back, stretching out he closed his eyes.

Pressing out the cigar butt in the ashtray, Roberto dialled another number to one of his associates. "Come on pick up," he said as he leaned back in his chair. It was close to 10:00 p.m., if nothing else he'd at least get an answering machine.

Finally, it was picked up on the other end. "Hello. Codwell, Budaka, & Francois Associates, can I help you?"

"Is this Foster Codwell?"

"Yes it is."

"Hey Foster, this is Roberto."

"Roberto, how are things? What a pleasant surprise; how are things proceeding in the Purgatorys."

"That's why I'm calling. Sorry for it being so late."

"No, no problem."

"Thank you. Listen I'm having a heck of a time trying to convince Cameron Kane to sign the contract. As you know, he's the only one in this area qualified or crazy enough for the job, but he doesn't want to budge. We sent a couple of trucks up to the Purgatorys, but the road only goes so far, and it's a piece of crap. It's going to take another four weeks before it'll be passable and even then we won't get much done without using the air. It looks like we're going to be set back a few weeks in development. In the meantime, I'm looking for another agency. We might be able to pull one out of Alberta. The only thing is, not sure any of them would qualify. The Purgatorys are a tricky place to land. There aren't many pilots around who want to attempt it. Cameron was, or is, our best chance. He's got both a plane and a helicopter, both of which we'll likely need as we progress."

"Can we afford the set back? A few weeks is a large chunk of change."

"Nope, probably we can't afford it. The thing is there's nothing we can do. Any news on what's happening in Ottawa on the land development proposal?"

"Not really. All systems point to go. Word is though that some of the Ktunaxa elder's and Tribal Council, are planning a visit to Ottawa themselves. Not sure what the potential threat is, minor I anticipate."

"Humph, that's never any good. They managed to convince legislation to put a halt to this the last time in '88. If we lose this opportunity, we'll be finished. We might have to resort to other means. Has any one made contact with that reporter, what's his name?" Roberto questioned as he tapped his finger on the edge of his desk.

"Bryce Ellwood. You probably recall a few of his articles. He's that *never give up* freelancer that put a halt to the three developments up in the East Kootenay that we were affiliated with. I can't remember the name he uses when he writes for Kootenay Leaf & Outdoor. He's always got articles in there. Good ones too," Foster remarked.

"Yeah, I recall. There's no news then on what he has or hasn't submitted yet?"

"Nothing so far. I'll be keeping my eyes open though. If we don't come up with something concrete from Ottawa before his contract expires up there and he's done his research, we might be in trouble."

"True enough." Roberto inhaled deeply then sighed. "Okay, Foster. I guess that's about it. I just wanted to check in. I'll talk to you again in a week or so."

"Indeed, Roberto. Talk to you then." The two hung up their phones.

Roberto pulled out another cigar from his shirt pocket, bit off the end and spat it on the floor. He had three problems now. One, the pilot Cameron Kane, two, the freelance writer Bryce Ellwood, and three, an unspecified number of irate Ktunaxa. All three added up to lost time and money, neither of which Robertar & Robertar Land Development, could afford. If they were unsuccessful in their second attempt in developing the Purgatorys, they'd be bankrupt in less than five years. Roberto inhaled a lung full of cigar smoke... *Hmmm, other means,* he thought.

Chapter 16

At 6:15 a.m., the following morning, Cam stepped out of the Yellow Mantis and walked the short distance to Jackson's office and cargo depot. Jackson was already seated behind the desk with a cup of hot coffee in his hand. "Good morning, Cam."

"Good morning, Jackson," Cam responded reaching for a Styrofoam cup. "Have the guy's started packing up Bryce's supplies yet?"

"Soon enough they will. Probably have the cargo loaded in an hour. How did you sleep last night?" Jackson asked as he shuffled through some paperwork on his desk.

"Like a baby with my eyes closed. Got another offer from Roberto, he upped the contract fifty grand. I'm still not interested though."

"He'll keep hounding you. He knows you're the only one good enough to fly in that area. He's no dummy. He didn't get to where he is today without a good head on his shoulder. Probably a lot of pushing too. Be careful of him."

"Ah, he can kiss my behind." Cam waved his hand through the air. "I didn't get to where I am today either, without a good head on my shoulders and a lot of guts." Cam chuckled as he pulled up to Jackson's desk. "He offers me a million and a half, I might consider it."

"Stand firm and he just might."

"I hope not. I hope he gets the hint. I'm not interested. I've lived here all my life. Have hundreds of flying hours to my credit all done in the four-corners of the Kootenay's and afar. I love these mountains, and I can't see myself being subjugated to helping Roberto and his company ruin them." Cam took a swig from his coffee, "Then again, a million and a half in US is a lot of cash. I might have second thoughts," he joked. The truth was, even then he wouldn't give in. No amount would change his mind.

"Paper work is all in order Cam. I need your John Henry here, and I'll see how far along the fellows are in sorting the cargo out. You are aware the supplies aren't scheduled for delivery until the 10th, aren't you?" Jackson asked as he rose.

"Sure am. I have another pressing engagement near that date. I figure Bryce will hear the plane. If he isn't around, I'll make sure to get the cargo up to his camp. No worries there."

"All right then. I don't see a problem."

"Thanks a lot, Jackson." Cam thumbed through the papers, adding his signature where needed. Standing himself, he walked over to the coffee urn, and poured another cup of the black plasma. He looked at his watch and did some calculating on his time frame. He still had the flight back to Cranbrook; then he'd have to unload the Yellow Mantis and load up the Kootenay Green. If he got away from New Kootenay at 7:30 a.m., and was lucky enough, he might wrap up the delivery to Bryce by 2:00 p.m., that afternoon. A busy day lay ahead. Cam took a drink from his coffee as Jackson returned. "What's the word?"

"She's all loaded and ready."

"Excellent. Thanks a lot. I'll get back to you later this afternoon. I'll fill you in on how Bryce is getting along." Cam began to exit the office.

"I'll be expecting a call. Thanks Cameron."

"You bet, talk to you soon." Exiting he looked to the early morning sky. It was a beautiful pale blue, the sun bright and hot. *A great day for flight,* he thought as he walked the short distance to the Yellow Mantis. In moments, the helicopter came to life as the rotors whirled, and Cam took to the skies.

Forty minutes later he was setting the helicopter down on his agency's landing strip ten miles north of Cranbrook, which sat on the shores of a man-made lake, all owned by Cameron Kane himself. As the rotors wound down, he stepped out and crouched, darting the distance to his office. His fax went off the moment he stepped in, and the phone began to ring. Tossing the paper work in his hand to the pile, he let the phone ring, stepping over to the fax to retrieve the transmission, he pressed the receive button. *Haven't even been here two minutes,* he thought.

Stepping back he turned and exited the office, walking the short distance to where his plane 'The Kootenay Green,' was docked and waiting for refuelling. His mechanic, receptionist and student pilot, weren't due until 10:00 a.m.; so rather than wait, he wanted to get a head start on the day. He checked over the plane, refuelled it, and was getting ready to load it with the cargo from the Yellow Mantis, when his mechanic showed up earlier than scheduled. "Glad I caught you before you decided to head out. The Kootenay is scheduled for a fuel system overhaul."

"Is it that time already?"

"Yep."

"Can it wait Pat? I need to get some stuff to Bryce at Leroy Lake."

"Damn it, Cam, you're the one who schedules these things. I hate leaving it for another day." There was a pause as Pat stroked his whiskered chin. "Leroy Lake isn't that long of a haul. How much does the cargo weigh?"

"A wild guess would be close to three, maybe four hundred pounds, plus or minus. I'd have to look again at the invoice."

"As long as you're not hauling six hundred plus I'd say you have about four hours of flight left on the carburettor before it kicks. I guess it's up to you to decide."

"Four hours is plenty of time. No problem then. Good, how about giving me a hand loading up?" Cam stepped off the plane.

"I suppose," Pat commented. "I'll grab the Kubota and trailer."

Two hours later, at 11:30 a.m., Cam was jetting across the lake the plane's engine full bore as it took to the skies.

Around the same time, Bryce and Redeemer were traversing the last mile of rough terrain along the creek before it opened up and became easier. They hiked a good distance that day, and their chances were good that they might make Leroy Lake by early evening, providing Bryce's leg held out. He leaned his weight onto the crutch to catch his breath. The truth was even now his leg hurt so badly that his teeth ached. He was beginning to doubt he could go further.

Grimacing, he stepped forward. "Come on, only a bit longer and the terrain will ease up." The cub darted ahead, thrashing in the creek as he did so. "I agree with you there. If I had it in me, I'd join you in a swim. It's certainly warm enough today." Chuckling Bryce hobbled passed him. They coursed their way over a couple more knolls until finally the easier terrain he'd been praying for, came into view. Hobbling to a clearing, he sat to catch his breath, when the distant drone of an approaching plane, broke the silence. Tilting his head, he listened intently, how he hoped it wasn't who he thought it was. Wincing in pain he rose and looked to the skies. Redeemer who was nearby, was looking to the heavens as well. Standing on his hind legs, his head perpendicular with his body as he gazed up he became dizzy and tumbled backwards. Bryce only caught a glimpse of the blunder, chuckling as he continued looking to the horizon. Finally he saw it, and sure enough, it was The Kootenay Green, Cameron Kane's bush plane. He knew there was no way they could make it back before it landed.

He brushed the back of his hand across his brow. *For a man whose claim to fame is 'never early, never late', he sure hasn't been living up to that these past few trips,* Bryce reminisced. *I'll fire a round or two from the rifle once he lands; maybe he'll hear it. Could try to signal him as he passes by on his return. That would be the best bet. A fire and smoke might work.* He looked around for some damp moss and green twigs, anything that would cause smoke. His legged bellowed in pain, but he desperately needed to stop Cam. Time dragged on. The audible din from the plane became silent. Cam had landed.

The Kootenay Green floated effortlessly across the mirrored surface of Leroy Lake, causing little waves too lap at the shore. Cam shut the engine down as the plane glided the last few yards to the shore. The camp sat silent, not a soul around. Stepping out of the plane, he deeply inhaled. *It doesn't look like anyone has been here in a while,* Cam thought.

Opening the cargo door, he unloaded the supplies on the shore then he called Bryce's name, but he got no response. In the distance, he thought he heard a rifle shot and he stood steadfast, waiting for another. Nothing sounded. Cam scratched the top of his head. *Best get the supplies up to the tent.*

Three miles north-east of Leroy Lake, Bryce was having trouble trying to fire another shot. The rifle jammed and now he struggled with removing the spent cartridge stuck in the chamber. *Seems as though if I didn't have bad luck, I'd have no luck at all. Instead, better get a flame to that fire,* he hobbled over to the pile of moss, twigs, and branches, but his luck didn't improve, as he tried to get the pile of twigs to take on a flame. It was no use, as the wood wouldn't light.

Cam, by now, was carrying the last box of supplies up to the tent; setting it down he stepped inside. It looked as it did the last time he was there, except it was cold and silent. Exiting, he hollered out Bryce's name. Getting no response, he looked around. *Maybe I should do a quick fly around, could be he's in trouble somewhere,* he thought as he traipsed back to The Kootenay Green. Firing up the plane's engine he glided across Leroy Lake taking on speed as he proceeded eastward. With only a few minutes to waste, he circled the vicinity a few times, keeping his eyes peeled for any sign of Bryce. It was hopeless. He saw nothing.

The sound of the plane was close now. Looking to the sky, Bryce waited to get a glimpse of the plane as it passed overhead. If nothing else, he could at least wave his arms. Cam though didn't fly overhead; instead he headed due east, straight back to Cranbrook. Bryce listened as the sound of the plane became distant then vanished completely. "That's it then, he's gone, looks like we'll have to contact someone as soon as we get back. Too bad I lost the cell phone. Not much we can do about that though," he sat in deep contemplation, his head resting in his hands.

Redeemer sat close, his big brown eyes looking into Bryce's own. "Ah, we'll manage. I missed the plane, that's not a big deal. I'll be able to contact someone back at camp. No use in crying over spilled milk. We'll set off again in a few minutes," he put his arm over Redeemer's broad shoulders, sighing as he looked up to the sky. *Will my luck ever change,* he wondered? Minutes passed until finally he found his strength once more, and slowly rose. "C'mon, lets head for camp."

Hayden Rochsoff and his wife, Colleen, were sitting at the kitchen table when Hayden's cell phone began to ring. Hayden hated the damn thing. Now as it rang, he looked on as though he wanted to smash it. "Well," Colleen started as she looked across the table to Hayden. "Aren't you going to answer?" she asked.

"Nah. They can leave a message." Hayden stood from the table and walked away.

"What if it's important?" Colleen reached for the phone herself, but it was too late. "There is a message, want me to get it?" Colleen looked at the cell phone screen. "It's a private number, no name."

"In that case, forget it. I'll listen to it later," Hayden responded from the back deck. Leaning against the railing, his mind lapsed into a time he wished he could forget. Two years earlier, in 2002, Colleen was kidnapped and held for a hefty ransom of twenty-million-dollars. He knew that ordeal could have played out differently, and both of them could be dead. Resolving the threat himself, he was forced to kill the two men involved. He'd been bruised, beaten, and scarred, but was never charged with any offence, as it was evident in Canadian law that he acted in self-defence when the two men died. That time still haunted Hayden. Inhaling deeply, he looked toward the forest that skirted their cabin. How he loved Deer Brook. It was a place where dreams were made, *at least his and hers.* Even during the worst of times, this was *always home.*

In his late thirties, he was in exceptional health. His dirty-blonde, shoulder length hair gently blew in the mid-afternoon breeze. His blue eyes were a testament to what he had been through. His wife Colleen was as athletic as the first day he laid eyes upon her. *She was still Colleen, brave and unstoppable.* Hayden often wondered if she too thought about that time, that time he desperately wished he could forget. They took an oath years earlier not to speak about the incident; *so far neither had.*

Their cabin in Deer Brook was situated on a bluff that overlooked the Arrow Lake. The land Hayden owned was vast and rugged, the way he liked it. They generated their own power with a big diesel generator, and their water came from a well. Not until recently did they even have a phone. Their cabin was a fortress.

Hayden was the sole proprietor of 'The Interior & Beyond Hunting Co.' He often wondered if he had more clients than he wanted, or for that matter needed. It was likely that the call he received earlier was someone seeking his expertise to charter an early spring bear hunt. He received five calls a day in that regard. Hayden's reputation as a hunting guide spoke for itself. His outfit was noted as one of the best in Western Canada.

As the wind picked up, Hayden could hear the waves of the Arrow Lake smashing against the rocks below their cabin. Leaving the deck, he followed the path that led to a bench where he could look out across the Arrow. Sitting down, he watched as the choppy waters lapped at the shore and bluff below. Seagulls dove and fluttered above the wakes, hoping for a feeding of fish. Their calls echoed although they seemed to be miles away. Hayden watched with content as he reminisced.

A half a mile east of Leroy Lake, Bryce and Redeemer were making their final leg to camp. "There it is, Redeemer, there it is." Bryce inhaled deeply. He had thought he was never going to make it back. The pain in his leg was excruciating, yet he sauntered on. Help and camp were within his sight, and he was going to make it there before he passed out from the pain. Redeemer, now aware of camp himself, dashed ahead, stumbling as he went. "That a boy, clear out any vagrants." Bryce found the humor to chortle as he watched the bear cub skirt home and undoubtedly look for food.

Minutes later he made the distance himself, and

slumped down at the picnic table. Taking note that the boxes Cam left behind only hours earlier; were intact and untouched, he sighed. "Really pushed it today, paying for it now." He wiped his brow. His leg throbbed as never before. Unknown to him it was grossly swollen to twice its size. If it were a water balloon, it would have burst by now. Whatever the condition his leg was in, he knew he'd live to see another day. Help was only a few keystrokes away.

Forty-five minutes later, he found the energy to once more stand. Hobbling to the solar panel, he checked the connections and charging status, they were good to go. Adjusting the satellite, he made his way inside the tent. A musty damp smell enveloped him when he entered. Opening the tent flap fully for circulation, he looked around, noting that the tent hadn't suffered in his absence. Making his way across the room, he sat down at the table that doubled as his desk, and booted up his laptop.

The screen flickered, *windows blue* then opened. Accessing his address book he clicked on Jackson's name then wrote: *Send help ASAP. Leg is broken. Cell phone lost. Safe and sound at Leroy Lake for now. Hurry, Bryce E.* Carbon copying the email to the Kootenay Forestry Service as well, he looked the brief email over then hit the send button, watching as his only prospect in getting help disappeared into cyber space. *Hope they check their email,* he thought as he winced. Making himself comfortable, he waited. The hard plastic chair was more comfortable than the hard ground that over the past few days he'd been forced to sit on.

It was Redeemer's hot breath against his out stretched legs that woke him. He shuffled in the chair as he lazily opened his eyes. "Must've dozed off, eh? Thanks for waking me." Reaching over he scratched the cub behind the ear, as he averted his eyes to the screen. *Still no response.* Looking to the bottom right corner of his laptop he noted the time. He'd been asleep for two and half hours. It was now 6:00 p.m. "Not going to hear from anyone tonight, everyone has gone home by now."

He worked his good leg into a position where he could

stand. With the little amount of strength he could muster, he headed outside. Making his way to the food cache, he unlocked it and bent down to retrieve some canned goods and a bag of jerky. He hadn't the pain tolerance to search for anything specific; whatever he grabbed would have to do.

Securing the door and locking it, he rested a moment and shared some of the jerky with Redeemer. "Whew, I hurt something awful, something awful," he repeated. Sweat formed at his brow, and he felt feverish. He hoped it was because of his exhaustion. *Getting a fever now will certainly put a damper on everything else, making it all seem worse,* he thought, as he inhaled deeply, taking up his walking stick they walked the short distance back to the tent.

An hour later with his stomach full, he began to feel better. *There was a light at the end of the tunnel after all,* he thought, as his eyes averted toward the shore and clear blue waters of Leroy Lake. Redeemer with energy to spare frolicked nearby; every now and again he'd make his way back to Bryce and check in on him. He would sniff at the wound on Bryce's leg and lick it, usually Bryce chuckled, but tonight he shooed Redeemer away. The pain he felt was tenfold for some odd reason. Determined to find the answer, he managed to swing his leg up onto a block of wood, and fighting the agonising pain he removed the splint. It was the first time that he'd removed it completely.

Sucking in a deep breath of air, he looked the black and blue mess over. Surprised as he was, that the bone remained straight, he was disappointed and quick to realise that he could not twitch a toe. At further inspection, it looked as though he might have gangrene. At that moment he felt as though all hope was lost; he knew what that would mean. His heart sunk deep into his stomach, looking to the sky he shook his head. "Please don't be gangrene; please, don't be gangrene," he muttered beneath his breath. If it were, death was the only outcome, unless he could summon the courage to saw off his own leg, but he shuddered at the thought.

Minutes passed as he sat there, hopeless and in great pain. Taking a second glance, he realised that the splint had been too tight. Miraculously a fleshy colour was beginning to show above the blackest bruise, and the swelling in only the first few minutes, had lessened. His heart fluttered with relief, *it wasn't gangrene after all*. With that realisation; things were looking up. "Gave myself a scare, for a minute," he spoke loud enough for Redeemer to hear. "Thought I ended up with gangrene, in which case you'd have been welcome to feed off what might have still been good." Light heartedly he half chuckled.

Deep down he knew that might have been the case. Luckily it wouldn't be, not now, and hopefully not in a day or two either. He could handle the pain for at least that long, after that it would be too late for his leg to mend correctly. It had already been four days. He would live, but the leg would become a burden. The only way to correct it then would mean having it surgically broken once more. He shook his head. "Whatever lies ahead, I guess lies ahead. I'm sure by tomorrow Jackson will have got my email and help will be on its way. Which leads to you." he fell silent for a moment, "What will we do with you?" It was a harsh question, and one he couldn't answer. "Ah, another bridge we'll have to cross when the time comes. I can promise you this much, once it's all said and done I'll be back here before the end of May. Recovered completely or on a good mend, I have a contractual deal to fulfil and I intend on fulfilling it."

Redeemer, who was lying on the ground next to him, yawned, rolled over, and fell asleep. "That a boy, have a good night's sleep. I'll be heading that way soon enough, once I find the courage to stand." Wanting to kill some time, Bryce reached for, and was able to pull a couple of the boxes Cam left behind, close enough to go through, opening the boxes was a chore, but he managed. The first box held the boots and hiking shoes, he ordered, along with a list of other things. Because of the state he was in and the fluctuating pain that shot up and down his leg, it took him an hour to go through the two boxes; the others would have to wait.

Staring at the hiking shoes and with a great desire to try at least the one shoe on, he grimaced in pain as he removed the moccasin from his right foot. Slipping on the shoe he sighed, it was heaven. He wiggled his toes making them dance, pleased that indeed the shoe was a good fit. He slowly stood, deciding it was better to leave the splint off for one night, and instead wrap it with strips from one of the older sheets for his cot. He proceeded to the tent, partly closing the flap as he stepped in, leaving enough room for Redeemer to make his way in if he decided.

Hobbling to his cot, he slowly lowered himself into the sitting position. Making certain it remained sturdy, and that the pieces of wood he used to prop up the end of it hadn't moved since he'd last slept in it, he wiggled a bit. Satisfied all was safe and with diligence not to hurt his leg, he slowly swung around and stretched out his legs. Although indeed he was careful, there was no denying that he didn't feel it, and he winced in pain. Minutes passed, and all he could do at that point was lie still. Inhaling and exhaling deeply, he focused his mind onto other things. Eventually the agonising pain subsided, and he proceeded to wrap his leg with strips from the top sheet of his cot, without having to stand or leave it. The task done he laid back and closed his eyes.

Back in Deer Brook, Hayden sat down at the table in his den, the fire snapped and crackled in the river rock fireplace, casting eerie shadows on the wall of the darkened room. Reaching to his right, he turned on the reading lamp, picked up his cell phone, and retrieved messages. Two were unimportant. One was from Conrad Jackson back at the Kootenay Forestry. "Damn," Hayden spoke aloud.

"What's that Hayden?" Colleen questioned with curiosity.

"Ah, I missed a call from Conrad. He's out of the office for a week, said Cam delivered supplies up to Bryce at Leroy Lake, but Bryce wasn't around I guess and hasn't called in, nor can they call him, seems his cell phone isn't getting a signal, and his email is down." Hayden tapped his finger on the desk.

"Does Conrad have a reason to be concerned?"

"Sounded as though he did. Wants me to catch a

helicopter flight with Cam back up to the lake tomorrow, to see if all is well. I'm supposed to call Cam tonight for further details."

"That's not so bad. It is only what, a two-hour round trip? Besides, you need to get out, you're getting miserable." Colleen wrinkled up her nose as she teased him.

"Yeah, I suppose you're right. I haven't seen Bryce for a couple months, not since he headed up that way. Could probably get some fishing in, too," Hayden hinted.

"I doubt Cam will want to stay, he's busy this time of year."

"That's the problem. I wonder if I shouldn't drive up, could stay a couple of days then. Can't make it quite to the lake but I could make it to Toby Creek. Maybe even check in on Hector Foxeagle. Haven't seen him in a while either."

Colleen understood Hayden's need to get away and perhaps a couple days at Leroy Lake with his old buddy, would do him some good. "That's a thought. Do you have anything else lined up? Any guiding charters to fill?"

Hayden shrugged, "Kinda, sorta, maybe. Not really."

"What is that supposed to mean?" Colleen snickered.

"Old John from Castlebridge was expecting me to take him up the Columbia to do some Walleye fishing. It's no big deal. He wasn't paying me. I figure he wanted to have some company."

"That's easy to fix. I wouldn't mind going to Castlebridge myself. Do some shopping and visit some friends. I could stop off and let him know you needed to go up and check on Bryce. He'll understand."

Hayden sat in contemplation. Walleye fishing did sound tantalising. The big picture was that he still needed to go up to Leroy Lake, regardless. "All right, sounds good. Thanks, Colleen. I appreciate it. Let John know that once I get back, we'll reschedule."

"Sure thing. No problem. What are you waiting for? Shouldn't you be packing?" Colleen jostled. "You could get out of here early tomorrow morning. Besides, the Siberian Tiger hasn't bush dogged in a while." she said, referring to

Hayden's 4x4, a 1968 Dodge Power Wagon. Hayden had built it from the frame up, midnight black in colour with a custom paint job of a Siberian Tiger on the hood, drawn by one of Colleen's artist friends. The truck was the envy of most. It was equipped with a two 5 ton winch system, one at the back and one in the front, CB and two-way radio equipped, and as recently as a week ago, a GPS was installed.

Under the hood was a blue printed 360 racing engine, compressor, and battery charging system. Hayden even built a few concealed cargo compartments for extra gear, guns, or whatever one's heart might desire. A four-inch custom-built black chrome roll bar and bush-guard highlighted the step side short box truck. The cargo box in the back, held survival equipment and an array of air powered tools. The truck was unstoppable. That and their cabin were Hayden's pride and joy. Neither of which he ever stopped working on.

Hayden nodded his head. "Yeah, I suppose you're right. You don't mind then that I take off for a day or two?"

"Hell no," Colleen chortled. "You need to get out for a while. Look at how antsy you've been. I could probably use some time out as well. That's why while you're gone, I'm going to go shopping in the big city of Castlebridge." Colleen chuckled as she stood up from the couch and walked over to Hayden. "Come on, let's get you packing. It's 9:00 p.m. already, and if we're going to do the *nasty* later we better get the packing out of the way." Reaching out her hand she took Hayden's and led him to the bedroom. "You get your clothes and gear and I'll pack food in the cooler. How many days will you be gone, do you think?"

"Two, three days at most. Unless of course something has happened to Bryce, possible, but not likely," Hayden responded.

Colleen stood in the bedroom doorway, "All right. I'll pack enough for three or four days."

"Thanks." Hayden made his way over to their closet and pulled out his packsack, it took a few minutes to throw some clothes in it and only a few more for Colleen to pack some of Hayden's favourite camp foods. By 10:00 p.m.,

Hayden was packed and ready. He even managed to contact Cam and told him about his plans. At 10:15 p.m., Hayden and Colleen were lying on their king-size pole frame bed. *It was time to get nasty.*

Chapter 17

Bryce slowly rose from his cot. He hadn't slept well at all. The pain he felt prevented that. The few times he managed sleep, it wasn't long before his leg throbbed, undaunted and constant. He was tired, hurt, and needed help, that was obvious. Hobbling to his laptop, he booted it up. "No response from Jackson yet." he mumbled. Looking at the time he realised it was 4:00 a.m. *No wonder,* he thought as he stood and exited the tent. The morning was brisk, dew from the night before made the grass and ground glisten in the early twilight. It looked as though it rained. Making his way over to the picnic table, he sat. It was going to be a long day.

Swivelling around he parked his legs beneath the table. The camp stove was comfortably within his reach. Giving it a few quick primer pumps, he lit it. Luckily, drinking water remained in the five-gallon container that sat on the table. It was a few days old, but drinkable. Turning the spigot he added water to the coffee-pot, swirled it around then dumped it. Rinsed out now, he made coffee and waited for the sun to rise. Two cups of coffee later he stood, and on a hunch headed inside to once more check his email. A response from one email simply stated that the email address was unknown. He looked the email over more closely. It was from the Kootenay Forestry Service, not from Conrad Jackson. *Thank God for that,* he thought.

According to the clock on his laptop, the time was now 5:15 a.m. A minimum of three hours would have to pass before Jackson gathered his email. He winced as he stood, making his way back outside. Redeemer was nearby, "Morning, how are you today? I'm struggling. Leg hurts like all mighty. To make things worse I got an email back from the ISP, apparently the Forestry Services email address is defunct, leastwise the one I have is. If I don't hear back from Jackson, I'll try to contact help via the Internet," he said with hesitation.

Bryce inhaled deeply. He wasn't Internet savvy. He knew how to use email, text messaging with his cell phone, and a fax, but unfortunately his laptop was not equipped for transmitting faxes, and his cell phone was long lost. Rarely did he cruise the net. It seemed intimidating to him, and he hated it as much as the pain he was feeling. The only two email addresses he had in his address book were Conrad Jackson's and the Kootenay Forestry, which was now defunct, or so it appeared. There were only two choices left if Jackson didn't send help or contact him. He'd either look for help on the net, or try and hike the ten miles to Hector's cabin at Toby Creek. The hike would take him as many days as there were miles, and by then it wouldn't matter, he'd be crippled. His best bet, he realised, was to sit tight and pray Jackson sent help. If no help came in the next while then he'd have no other choice but to summon up assistance via the World Wide Web.

Early that morning at 5:30 a.m., Hayden left for Leroy Lake, unbeknownst to Bryce. Without any means to contact him, there was no way to let him know. At 8:00 a.m., Hayden pulled off onto a forestry road that led to Toby Creek and Hector Foxeagle's cabin. It was a twenty-five minute drive and the road rarely used, was overgrown, rough and muddy. Hayden's Siberian Tiger on a few misguided zigs and zags, on occasion slipped and slid. Scraping into the overgrowth of willow that jutted out onto the road, leaving a few noticeable scratches on both the driver's side and the passenger's side of Hayden's pride and joy, he cursed some, but continued. The scratches were nothing he knew he couldn't buff out and touch up. Coming to the fork in the road, he followed the lower one, which led to Hector's cabin and eventually Leroy Lake. Stopping a short distance from the fork he stepped out and stretched his legs.

From where he parked to Hector's cabin, was five miles he guessed. Looking around he inhaled the fresh brisk spring air and poured himself a coffee from his thermos. Leaning against his truck, he admired the scenery. The trees were green and plush. The mountains that formed the Purgatory's at their peaks and from what he could see of them were capped with snow. Everything was in its glory and he loved it all. Finishing the last of his coffee, he climbed back into his truck and with one last glance around, headed for

Hector's and Toby Creek.

At Leroy Lake, Bryce was realising why his emails hadn't been answered. His laptop was acting up and wouldn't accept certain key commands. He was stranded; there was no doubt about it. He shook his head at this discovery and the fact that he depended on the technology. In earlier times, ten or fifteen years prior, there would have been no way he would have relied upon it. Now as he sat there feeling stranded, miserable and in great pain, it failed him and now more than ever, he needed it to work. "Damn it," he drew in a deep breath.

With no communications to the outside world, his only choice was to head for Hector's place, a ten-mile jaunt that might see him to his grave. *Got to do what I got to do I guess,* slowly standing, he took up his walking stick and grabbing his first aid kit he headed outside to gather what little amount of gear he could handle. Redeemer, being as curious as he was, darted to his side. "And what might I be doing, you ask?" he joked as he looked at the cub with a weak smile. "Truth is, we have to make our way to Hector's cabin. Any communications I had are gone. My laptop seems to have given up the ghost."

Tossing the first aid kit onto the picnic table, he sat. If he was going to hike, he needed to put a splint back on his ailing leg. Raising his leg, he gently set it onto the block of wood he used earlier. The pain was torturous, and he sucked in a lung full of air. "Damn. That hurt." Tears streamed down his cheeks from his watering eyes to the corners of his mouth. There was no way he'd even make a half a mile a day, and he knew it. He decided to stay put and try to get some communications back online. At least where he was he had shelter, food and water. Eventually someone was bound to come by. He didn't have gangrene, and he knew he wouldn't die from a broken leg, but getting stuck out in the mountains was another story.

The next thing he remembered was waking up as the hot late morning sun beat down on his face. Either he'd passed out from the pain or exhaustion, whatever the case he obviously passed out. Rubbing his eyes, he looked around as he slowly came awake. His leg he noticed, was still stretched out across the block of wood, and by all accounts felt a lot better. Redeemer was nearby sleeping on his old sweater and Leroy Lake was as placid as a painting.

He decided then and there that indeed his best bet was to stay put and to do what he could to try and get back online. It was likely a simple glitch. With some patience and a diligent effort, he might be able to correct the problem. If not, at least he was safe and would live through the ordeal.

By now, Hayden was sitting with Hector and Rayne, drinking coffee and eating cornmeal biscuits. Their reunion lasted an hour and the three conversed on everything and nothing at all. Realising the time, Hayden rose from the table. "It's getting on to be 10:00 a.m., Hector, Rayne. I best get going if I want to make it to Leroy Lake."

"Are you sure you don't want Rayne to double you in on her horse?"

"Nah, I appreciate the offer, but I kind of want to surprise him. I should stroll into his camp near suppertime if I leave now. It's the best time to do some fishing." Hayden smiled.

"It is a nice hike, especially at this time of year. When you return in a few days, you will stay for coffee and cakes, won't you?" Rayne questioned.

"Most certainly. Thank you, Rayne." Hayden stepped off the porch, waving as he walked back to his truck and grabbed his gear. Checking it over, he threw the pack over his shoulder and headed toward Leroy Lake. Non-the wiser in knowing that Bryce had broken his leg; just as Bryce was none the wiser in knowing that Hayden was coursing his way to Leroy Lake.

He walked non-stop until it was noon, the whole time reminiscing about his childhood, and the village of Poski, where he grew up. The terrain there was much like it is here in Canada, the only difference was that in Russia it was colder and winters were longer. As he thought back, he was relieved that he was one of a very few who were ever truly free from the communism of his youth. Although he had seen a lot of bloodshed that he himself was a part of, Hayden Rochsoff was truly free. Canada was his home now, and he loved and honoured it as the great country that it was. Russia to him was a distant memory.

Finding shade beneath an evergreen tree, he removed his pack and sat down for a break. Removing the soft-sided cooler from the top of his pack he grabbed a V8, opened it, and slugged it back. He wasn't quite hungry, not after eating the three or four cornmeal biscuits back at Hector's. He drank another V8 then tossing the pack over his shoulder he set off once more. He guessed Leroy Lake to be six miles away. Only a few more hours and he'd be casting his line into the lake and bullshitting with Bryce. He was excited about the whole ordeal, could hardly wait to make the distance.

Trudging forward, he took in all the sounds, the rustling of leaves and branches as the breeze gently caressed them. The sounds of birds as they chorused, were all familiar sounds. If it wasn't Heaven, he didn't know what it was, except that being alive never felt so good, and he smiled.

Bryce was doing all he could to solve his communications problem. His laptop still wouldn't take any commands. Every now and again, it would flicker then shut off. Dealing with the pain in his leg and the stupid laptop, was proving to be the makings of a very unproductive day. Anything and everything he tried, both to subdue the pain and to get back online was fruitless.

By 3:00 p.m., he gave up once more on the laptop, and the excruciating pain that shot bolts of lightning up and down his leg, didn't help matters. Finally sitting back outside with his leg outstretched, he was able to think clearly. He had done everything he knew how to do, but the laptop wasn't co-operating. There had to be something he was missing, something probably so simple that it would make his head spin once he realised what it was. Absorbing the hot rays from the sun, he contemplated. *What am I missing?*

Two miles north-west of Bryce's camp Hayden was taking another well-deserved break. He had made good time. In another hour, maybe two, he'd have full view of Leroy

Lake and the camp at which Bryce was staying. Resting, he took the opportunity to fulfil a nasty craving from a habit he'd recently taken up, removing from his shirt pocket a package of Colt Mild Cigars, eight in a box. A box of eight lasted him over a week and he still had six left.

Putting the wine tipped Colt between his teeth, he drew a match across its striker and inhaled the pungent smoke. It tasted and felt good as the smoke filled his lungs; exhaling, he coughed for a moment then inhaled again then he stood. A bit dizzy from both the heat and cigar, he shook his head, wondering why he ever took up the habit. It wasn't as though he smoked them every day or even inhaled the smoke more than twice from each one he lit. The rest of the time he let them burn out and chewed on the tip. It was a poor excuse on why he continued, and he knew it.

Pressing the cigar out, he stuck it back in the box with the others, looked in the direction of Leroy Lake, and sauntered on. He walked steadily for almost two hours when finally the camp came into view. Stopping he looked on. It didn't appear as though anyone was near. The camp was completely silent, almost ghostly. Then he saw it, a grizzly cub. His heart sped up and skipped a beat. His only thought was that Bryce had become dinner. Hayden approached closer, unarmed and concerned at what he might be coming into. Regardless though, he knew he must find out. Removing his pack for more agility in case he needed to run, Hayden set it on the ground and with only his fishing knife in hand, he inched his way closer.

The cub had noticed him and it darted behind the tent. Looking in all directions, Hayden stood motionless amongst the shadows. His eyes caught movement from inside the tent, and he waited. *Could it be the cub's mother,* he thought as he looked on, preparing himself for what might happen next. Finally he saw Bryce hobbling out. Fearing now for Bryce's life that the mother bear was near, Hayden hollered aloud and grabbing his pack ran forward. "Bryce get away from there, a bear is behind the tent. Hurry," Hayden's voice boomed as he approached.

Startled, Bryce spun around to see who was addressing him, wincing in pain when he twisted his leg. Realising it was Hayden, he hollered back. "Hayden, no worries, it's only an orphaned cub, his name is Redeemer." Hobbling over to the picnic table, he sat down, as Hayden made the distance.

"What do you mean an orphaned cub?" Hayden started as he realised that Bryce wasn't well. "That's a heck of a mess. How long has it been like that?" Hayden questioned referring to Bryce's leg. The cub issue seemed less important now.

"Seven days tomorrow. Hurts like almighty too."

"I bet it does. We got to get you out of here. Jackson wasn't sure if something happened to you or not, after you didn't report in for a day or two, he asked me to fly here with Cam. Sorry about that, Bryce, I assumed you were fine so I drove to Toby Creek." Hayden inhaled deeply. "I feel bad, Bryce, sorry," he looked closer at Bryce's leg. "I guess hiking out was out of the question?"

"Yep. I lost all my communications too. If I could only get my damn laptop online, again I could email for help, unless, of course you have a cell phone?" Bryce questioned with optimism.

"Nope. I brought nothing like that. My truck is parked over at Hector's and I have two way radio communications with Colleen back at Deer Brook and a CB, I could hike back and radio ahead? Wouldn't get there before tomorrow, don't think I could make as good time coming here as I'll make going back, especially if I were to leave now. Maybe together, we can figure out the laptop issue. If not, I'll head back to Toby Creek early tomorrow." Hayden set his packsack down.

"I guess that's the only option for now. All right, give me a minute to catch my breath. You scared me some, and I twisted the leg a bit."

"Scared you? Ha, I was more scared then you when I saw that cub. Thought for sure you were lunch." Hayden chuckled. "All I had to avenge your mortal soul was my fishing knife. Now wouldn't that have been a sight. A dinky knife against a pissed off mother grizzly; don't think I'd have stood a chance," he recounted with humor as they began to chuckle. "Least you have a sense of humor still. That's always a good sign."

"Like you, I've learned that certain situations that aren't preventable, are no reason to lose hope, faith and even humor. I'd be dead by now if I let all those things go. You have to keep your wits about you, stay alert and play the cards that are dealt to you." Bryce rose from the table. "Let's see what we can make of that laptop," he said as he opened the tent's flap and walked in. Hayden followed. "Here it is. Every time I boot up, she works for a minute and goes cold." Bryce booted it up. They waited. The screen flickered then went black. "See, she does that to me every time." Bryce shook his head.

"Is all your data backed up?"

"It is."

"All right then here is what you need to do, restart it and go into DOS, key in FDISK, when the screen flickers and before it goes into windows, hit delete and go into advanced set up. Essentially what we'll be doing is swiping her clean and reinstalling all the drivers etc, that is of course if we can get that far, and you have all the drivers and such on CD."

"I do. Got them all right here." He tapped on the CD case that held all his floppies, CD's and such. "I've never done what you're asking me to do though. Maybe you want to do it?"

"I've never done it either, only watched Colleen. It's the blind leading the blind, Bryce. It's our only hope of getting it up and running, unless you know of some other way. You've picked up a virus or something. Maybe lost some DLL files. Don't ask me what those are either, cause I don't know."

"All right, here it goes." Bryce restarted the laptop in DOS and followed Hayden's instructions. In two hours after swiping the laptop and reinstalling windows, as well as all the drivers, the laptop issue was solved and his communications were back online. "Excellent. Now to send off an email and hope like hell we get a response in the next while."

"You might want to send that email to Cam. Jackson is

out of the office for a week. Heck better yet, send it to Colleen. Hayden told Bryce her email address and in a blink of an eye it was sent, twenty minutes later they got a response. Colleen contacted Cam by phone and he was heading their way. It was only a matter of time before help arrived.

They waited close to an hour before the sound of a helicopter echoed in the distance. Fifteen minutes later Bryce was on his way to the Kootenay Hospital. Hayden agreed to stay behind to hold the fort down until Bryce got a clean bill of health and made his return, in likely two weeks they assumed. Although he wouldn't be able to walk without crutches, Bryce was determined to fulfil his contractual obligation. Hayden watched as the helicopter headed over the mountains and out of sight. *Two weeks of nothing but fishing,* Hayden thought as he looked toward Leroy Lake and smiled.

Chapter 18

The following morning, Hayden spent the better part checking out Bryce's camp, and trying to make friends with Redeemer. The bear cub was not co-operating though and he kept his distance, watching the strange new man from afar. Hayden finished his coffee and shrugged, *I'll carry on like he isn't there*. His rod in hand, he walked the short distance to the lake, found a place to cast his line in and settled for a day of fishing. Looking around he couldn't fathom why anyone would want to destroy such a prestigious ecosystem to throw up a ski resort. The longer he sat and the more he thought about it, the better he realised Bryce's determination to put a stop to it.

Feeling a tug on his line, he gave the fishing rod a jerk and began to reel it in. The fish, fighting and pulling, cleared the water in an attempt to escape the painful hook in its mouth, landing with a loud splash as it dove once more into the depths of Leroy Lake. Seeing and hearing this, Redeemer who was nearby, became curious and darted closer to the shoreline next to Hayden. "Hello there, cub. Interesting thing going on out there, isn't there?" Hayden continued fighting the fish as his rod bent and his reel whined. Landing the fish, he was surprised at the size. Three pounds he guessed. "Not bad for a first cast eh, cub," he said as he broke the fish's neck and set it in the cool water with a big rock on its tail.

Redeemer crawled closer as though there were a need to sneak up on it. He looked on, impressed at the fish and its size. Before Hayden could stop him, he grabbed the fish and headed for the shadows, leaving Hayden at the shore cussing him. "What? No kiss before you screw me, you little bugger," he said with a chuckle as he cast a second time. Not so lucky with his second cast, he pulled in a belittled twelve-inch lake trout, a wee version of what the cub ran off with. His luck didn't change that day and that little twelve-inch trout was his last catch.

Earlier that morning at the Kootenay General Hospital, Bryce was waiting for the surgeon. He was told the night before when he was brought in, that he suffered extreme nerve damage, and that, of course, during the time that elapsed since the break, the bone had fused together incorrectly, a prognosis that Bryce had already assumed. He was hoping the surgeon had better news.

There was a slim possibility that he'd be able to walk after it healed completely as it was now, although not as well. Otherwise, it would have to be surgically broken and set. It all came down to what the good doctor had to say. Bryce waited patiently with his fingers crossed. He dreaded the thought that they might have to go that route. He was halfway healed; to go through it all over again brought back the thought of the agonising pain when it was first broke. It would also set him back a good month on his research, something he hadn't counted on.

As he waited he made phone calls to Colleen and filled her in that Hayden stayed behind to watch over the place. He called Jackson at home and left him a message pretty much stating the same. He continued to wait, growing more impatient and fidgety as time passed. Finally, the doctor arrived. He introduced himself and explained what kind of break he had and that the nerve damaged he suffered wasn't permanent. He gave Bryce two alternatives: he could live with a mildly crooked leg which over the course of time would likely develop other symptoms such as arthritis, bursitis, and a few other 'itisis', or he could have the leg surgically broken and set correctly. The doctor informed him that no matter which choice he made, he had better prepare himself for weeks of physiotherapy. When asked how many weeks, the doctor simply said, 'eight'. Bryce almost fell off the bed. "Eight weeks?" he questioned with the hope that he misheard.

"Easily that long, but not before the cast gets removed, you'll have the pleasure of wearing one for about three weeks. Luckily overnight, the swelling went down enough. You'll only need to be bed ridden for three or four days if you leave it as it is. You did a pretty-good job setting it yourself, actually, other than the tibia being a bit crooked. I'll let you decide what you want to do, just keep in mind what I've said about the possibility of future symptoms. I'll be back in a couple of minutes." The doctor turned with Bryce's chart and exited the room.

No matter what, there are eleven weeks of hell ahead of me. Bryce sighed at the thought. That would take him right through until August, a month before his contract expired. He felt useless at that point. "What am I going to do? What can I do?" he whispered to himself as he contemplated what lay ahead. He decided then to leave the leg as it were, get it fitted with a proper cast, spend the three or four days laid up in bed then head back to Leroy Lake where he would hobble around and do what he could. It was his only option. There were things to do around the camp until the cast was removed. A lot of flora and fauna were in the vicinity, birds, squirrels, and the like. He could devote three weeks to that easily enough.

Not a few minutes, but an hour and a half later, the doctor returned. "Sorry about the delay, Mr. Ellwood."

Bryce looked on and shrugged, "That's all right. I've decided to have it fitted for a cast as it is. I'll deal with the other possible problems at a later date if they show up."

"That's fine. You'll of course have to sign a waiver stating that any other symptoms that arise from the injury do not reflect this Hospitals work ethics, and that you were well informed of future prognoses."

"By all means."

"All right then, I'll round the documents up and have a nurse come back to put you in a cast. I've also written you up a prescription for pain and inflammation." The doctor handed him the prescription, and exited, returning shortly he handed Bryce the waiver on a clipboard. Bryce nodded and signed the document. "Thank you Mr. Ellwood. The nurse should be by anytime now to get you in that cast. I'll stop off and see you tomorrow morning." he said as he exited.

Minutes later the nurse showed up. "Hello, how are things today?"

"Good as can be expected. Are you here to put a cast on my leg?"

"Sure am. Actually this one isn't the permanent one,

we can't do that until we can be sure that the cuts and abrasions don't get infected."

"How long will I have to wear this one?" he asked with little enthusiasm.

"Only while you're here, three or four days, we'll put the more permanent one on, the day before you leave. By the way, it was quite a nasty break, how did you manage to set it yourself?"

He tilted his head as he looked on and watched her. "Between two rocks if you can believe it."

"Ouch. That must have hurt," she responded as she continued wrapping his leg with cotton and plaster.

"I won't deny that." The room grew silent as the nurse finished up.

"There we go, all done. As it dries it will feel tight and you can bet it's going to get awful itchy in the days to come, but I think it will heal up nicely." She tapped Bryce on the wrist and exited. The cast went from his toes, to his thigh. Already it felt uncomfortable.

Reeling in his line, Hayden thought he heard a horse galloping in the distance. Looking westerly, he saw Rayne approaching, setting his rod down he walked back to the tent and waited for her to make the distance.

"Morning."

"Good morning. We heard a helicopter last night, is everything okay?"

"That depends, I suppose. Bryce was alive; he had a messed up leg though. The helicopter you heard was Cameron Kane. He air-lifted Bryce to the Kootenay General."

"What happened?" she asked with concern as she dismounted.

"Said he took a tumble over a waterfall, north of here at Jack Pine Creek. Spent a few days hiking back to only discover that all his communications were down."

"Why didn't he use his cell phone?" Rayne approached and sat at the picnic table.

"Lost it."

"The poor guy. I bet he was pleased to see you."

124

"He was. We spent a couple of hours swiping his laptop, got it up and running then emailed Colleen. She passed on the message to Cam. An hour or so later he showed. Bryce wasn't too talkative, being he was in some pain and all, but he did fill me in on a few things, like that cub of his." Hayden smiled as he looked toward Redeemer who was lying in the grass near the shore.

Rayne chuckled, "I guess you're keeping an eye on everything then?"

"Yeah, least until he gets back. Having some trouble, getting to know that cub. The little bugger took off with my biggest fish earlier."

"He's a little trickster. Bryce bit off more than he can chew I think. Still, I admire him for taking the cub under his wing. Poor thing would've died by now."

"That's to be debated," Hayden replied as he looked at Rayne. "I've heard of them surviving if they were orphaned in their first autumn." Hayden averted his eyes once more toward the cub. "It's rare, but it has happened." Sharing some coffee, the two friends reminisced.

"Least now I can tell Grandfather why we heard that helicopter; he thought it was that land developer."

"Robertar?"

"Yeah."

"Nah, he isn't going to try coming here yet. There's nothing he can do at the higher altitudes, too much snow up there. First thing they'll do anyway, is minor surveying. They can't do much else, until the forces that be give them the go ahead. I'm not so sure that's going to happen."

"I sure hope not. I'd hate to see all this go."

"No kidding." Hayden looked toward Leroy Lake and shook his head. "It's a crime that people like Robertar can't see the true beauty here. Instead, people like him only want to exploit places like this to line their own pockets. I really have no use for people like that."

"You and me both." Rayne stood from the table. "It's getting on to dusk, think I better head back."

Hayden nodded, "Yeah. I think I'm gonna try casting

my line one more time. Might get lucky and catch something other than a twelve-inch pan fry."

"Good luck." Rayne swung onto her horse, waved, and sauntered off. Hayden coursed his way back to his rod, took it up and cast out. He spent two hours trying to catch fish, but for some reason, they weren't biting. Returning to the tent, he made himself and Redeemer some food. It had been an interesting day, and as he looked westerly, he watched in awe as the sunset slowly gave way to a pitch-black night. Sipping coffee around the fire, he listened to the loons and frogs as they chorused. It was a symphony of haunting echoes, and he listened with satisfaction.

Chapter 19

Rising as the sun caressed the mountains, Hayden exited the tent. Redeemer as always, lay on his sweater outside. Hayden made his way to the picnic table, turned on the Coleman stove and perked coffee. Redeemer rolled over, looked at him, and with some interest approached.

"Good morning, cub. Looks to be the start of a hot day, doesn't it?" Hayden questioned as the cub got close. "Going to head back to the lake after some coffee and a bite to eat. Got plans today to catch a bigger fish than that one you snaffled from me yesterday. I'll even share it with you if you let me get it back here." He really didn't know if he was going to catch a bigger fish or not, but he did know that he was indeed going to go fishing. The coffee now perked and he poured himself a cup, bringing it to his lips he blew on it then took a sip.

"What should we throw into our gullets this morning, cub? Feel like some bacon? I even got a dozen fresh eggs, was going to cook them up for Bryce, knowing that all he's got are the dehydrated type. Since he isn't here, I guess that leaves you and me, and I feel like eggs and bacon." The camp filled with the scent and sound of sizzling bacon and eggs. A half-hour later satisfied and full, he grabbed his rod and tackle, and headed for the shores of Leroy Lake, Redeemer trailing close behind.

Not from the first cast, the second, or even the third, did he get so much as a nibble. Deciding after some time to use the canoe to get out further and maybe have better luck, he walked the short distance to where it sat on the shore. Turning it onto its keel, he looked the twelve-foot canoe over. It looked safe enough. Smiling, he picked it up and set it in the water. He looked out across the lake to near the middle. It was out there in the deep blue water, where he hoped to reel in a fish or two. Retrieving the paddle, his rod and tackle, he stepped into the canoe. The canoe glided across the water like no other canoe he'd ever paddled. In only a few strokes, he made the distance to near the middle of the lake. Letting the canoe glide on its own, he added a bob-float to the line, baited the lure with pieces of bacon left over from that morning, and cast his line in.

Reaching in to his shirt pocket he pulled out the package of Colt cigars, opening it he removed the one he started to smoke a few days earlier, stuck it between his lips, struck a match and inhaled a lung full of the acrid smoke. The sun beamed down on him hot and heavy, but it felt good; freedom always did. Averting his eyes toward the shoreline, he could see Redeemer, who sat vigilantly looking on. Smiling, he inhaled another lung full of smoke.

Turning his gaze now toward the bob-float a good sixty or seventy-feet away. He waited patiently for it to bob up and down, but nothing happened. Reeling in, he cast once more, only this time further out. In only minutes he felt and saw the tug on the line. Jerking it, he waited for a response. The line went taunt and rod bent then he heard the audible snap as the fish took off with his lure and bobber. He couldn't believe it. It was the first time in years that a fish had broken his line. Full of adrenaline he connected another hook, loaded it with bacon, cast near the same spot, and waited. Nothing came of the cast. After reeling the line in, he cast to the opposite side of the canoe near some lily pads. Again, nothing. He half chuckled. "Seems I've been skunked again."

Setting his rod down in the canoe, he paddled a few strokes further east. The sun was behind him now and the trees skirting the south shore, cast shadows across the lake where he finally decided to try his luck once more. Lucky he was. Casting in his line he jigged a couple of times, almost instantly the line went taunt. Giving it a quick jerk, he began to reel in. At first it went slack, and he thought he might have lost his catch then like a flash the line went taunt, the reel whined as the fish took off to depths unknown.

Quickly adjusting the reel's tension, he gave another quick pull, reeling slowly and constantly. The battle was on. It was a good fight too. For fifteen minutes, man and fish struggled against each other's strength. Hayden became the victor, finally reeling in the solid seven-pound monster bass. Clubbing it with the handle of his knife, he tossed it to the floor of the canoe. It hopped and skipped a bit until finally becoming still.

Hayden looked at the catch, "Since I was able to reel you in without you breaking my line, I guess that leaves Mr. Big Bass out there somewhere." Hayden looked out across the lake, *out there beneath the depths of this lake is one heck of a big fish,* he thought. Noting that the mosquitoes were starting to become a nuisance and that it would soon be dusk, taking his time, he paddled for shore. There was no need to catch any more fish. Seven pounds of gutted bass would be plenty for both him and Redeemer.

As he got closer to shore, the cub stood on his hind legs and looked on. His powerful sense of smell told him that in the bottom of the canoe was a fish, and he waited patiently, his head held high as he ruthlessly sniffed at the air. Docking the canoe, Hayden stepped out. "Check out supper, cub." Grabbing the fish by its gill's he lifted it out of the canoe. "Seven pounds I'm guessing, of monster bass," he looked at his catch. "There are even bigger ones out there. Nice, eh? We'll roast the entire thing over a flame I think. Might even decide to wrap it up with leafs and mud and maybe toss it right onto some coals."

He scratched his chin. "Not sure actually, how I'd like to fix it up, on a spit, in the coals, or fillets and steaks. We'll figure that out later." He pulled the canoe onto the shore. Gutting the fish, he tossed the innards to Redeemer who lavishly licked them up then, with rod, tackle and fish in hand, he walked back to the tent.

He set the fish down on the table and plastered it with salt and pepper. Letting it sit for a minute, he lit a fire. Deciding he'd roast it over the spit, he skewered it with a stick and set it on the flames of the fire. It didn't take long for the smell of the cooking fish to emanate the camp. Inhaling deeply, Hayden gave the spit a turn. Redeemer, finished with his treat down by the shore, now caught the scent of the roasting fish, and he scrambled for camp. If there was more, he wanted it.

Hayden was sitting next to the fire with a coffee in his

hand, when Redeemer made the distance. "Got a snout full, eh? Smells good doesn't it?" he questioned as the cub drew close, closer than ever before. "See I'm a friendly sort." He held out his hand, but Redeemer distanced himself. "I see, still aren't sure if you want to be friends or not huh?"

Hayden turned the spit once more. "That's all right; not sure I want to get too attached to you either. Cute as you are and all, I might want to take you home with me." He chuckled. *Wouldn't that be something, a fellow like me who hunts things like him, bringing him home.* He took a drink from the coffee in his hand.

A few moments later, Redeemer rose on his hind legs and looked toward the forest, his ears tilted back he dropped to all fours and dashed closer to Hayden and the fire then rose once more, skittishly looking on. Startled, Hayden looked in the same direction, but saw nothing, "What is it, cub? What do you see?" Paying close attention to anything that might move, he scanned the brush line. Whatever the cub was seeing, he wasn't.

Standing now, he squinted, despite the sun in his eyes, he thought he did see movement. Blocking the sun with his left hand, he was able to see what it was that startled Redeemer. Near the brush line, perhaps 300 yards away, routing through an old log, was a full-grown grizzly. An unwelcome presence indeed, Hayden turned toward the tent calculating the distance in case he had to make a run for Bryce's .308 that was inside. Satisfied he could make it if the bear decided to get cantankerous, he stood still.

The bear looked in his direction and sniffed at the air, undoubtedly smelling both the fish and the man. Hayden stood steadfast as the bear finally rose on its hind legs and glared at him. Rocking its head back and forth a few times, it dropped to all fours, made a fake dash forward then rose once more. That's all it took for Redeemer, who darted to the safety of the picnic table.

Hayden's heart was in his mouth. Beads of sweat formed on his brow. The bear was still 150 yards away. He knew if he were to run, the bear would charge, in which case he'd likely have to shoot it; that is, if he were given the chance and the bear didn't get to him before he got to the .308. Instead, he held his ground and started to yell, "Go away bear! Go on! Get out of here!" he repeated loudly as he waved his arms. The bear still on its hind legs, batted its big paw through the air, dropped to all fours, turned and dashed back into the woods. Hayden continued his gaze toward the forest where the grizzly had bolted into the undergrowth. His mouth was dry and his heart beat a mile a minute. He inhaled deeply. *Whew. That was unexpected. Glad he decided to head for the hills, least I hope that's where he headed.* Hayden looked back to the tent. Deciding not to take any chances, he walked the short distance and grabbed the .308, making sure it was loaded. He shouldered it and headed back to the fire and the roasting fish. Redeemer remained beneath the picnic table, hidden from sight, or so he thought.

Back at the fire, Hayden knelt down and gave the spit a turn. He tossed another stick in, bringing up the flames. Staying alert and ready, he cautiously scanned the darkening forest. Without as much as a warning Redeemer cried out in pain and fright, turning quickly Hayden saw the cause. The grizzly bear had circled around and was batting at Redeemer who swatted back.

Before he had a chance to fire the rifle, the entire table collapsed from the massive bear's weight and the cub was trapped beneath all the debris, obviously hurt as he cried out in pain. As the big grizzly continued excavating what was left of the table, trying desperately to get to him, a warning shot from the rifle pierced the evening. The massive bear startled, rose on its hind legs, and darted for the undergrowth, only to circle around one more time, and unexpectedly charged Hayden.

Only by chance did Hayden catch a glimpse of the charging bear. Raising the rifle to his shoulder another rifle blast echoed, and the massive bear stumbled then fell silent. Before he made the distance to where the dead bear lay, Redeemer rose from the debris, shook himself off, sniffed the air, and approached the still bear two steps ahead. "Don't know if that was the proper thing to do or not, cub." Hayden looked at the dead grizzly. "Damn thing charged me though, I had no choice," he knelt next to the carcass. "Going to have to report this." Looking on he pulled out his package of Colt cigars, put one in his mouth and lit it. Inhaling deeply, he sighed. *I can't figure out what made him act that way. Strange,* he thought as he drew in another lung full of smoke.

Redeemer, by now, had lost interest, and he lay nearby, shaken but not stirred. Standing, Hayden shouldered the rifle and walked back to the fire. The fish feast he was hoping for didn't seem as appealing as it once did. Regardless, he turned the spit as he gazed into the flames. The Colt dangling from his mouth, he reminisced about what had transpired and for the life of him, he couldn't understand the bear's aggressive attempted assault. He was glad about one thing, and that was that he'd retrieved the rifle when he had. Standing now, he took the stick off the spit. The big bass was cooked and ready for eating, and eat it they would.

Two hours later, full and content, Hayden gathered what was left of the picnic table and leaned the parts and pieces against a stump. He cleaned up what he could of the mess the bear had left behind. Making sure the Coleman stove hadn't suffered too badly, he lit it. Setting the table top onto some blocks of wood, he pulled a chair up to it; *it would do.* He put his hands behind his head, stretched out his feet, and looked to the evening sky. Another day had passed.

Chapter 20

Bryce lay on the hospital bed with his leg hanging from a sling held together by some contraption with springs and pulleys. It had been that way since he'd had the cast on. Now, three days later, that particular cast was to be removed, and the raw wounds on his leg were going to be checked. If all was well, he'd be fitted with a permanent cast until the bone mended; three weeks he'd been told. Then the tedious physiotherapy for the next eight weeks would begin. His hope was that the physiotherapist would give him a list of exercises that he could do on his own. That way he could continue with his work, rather than having to call it quits until the therapy was over. That wasn't for another three weeks at least. Until then he wouldn't worry about it.

At 8:00 a.m., the nurse arrived. "Good morning. How are we today?"

"I'll feel a lot better once this cast comes off, and you give me a clean bill of health." He winked at her.

"Let's hope I can do that for you." The nurse lowered his leg and cut away the cast. Pulling it apart, it broke into two pieces, and she tossed them into a bin. "You'll be pleased to know, everything looks good. There's no sign of infection, other than some continued swelling. I'd say you're good to go."

"Excellent! That makes my day."

"I can tell." The nursed smiled at him as she pulled the table holding the casting material, closer. "It won't be long now and we'll have this leg put into its home." She spoke as she continued wrapping his leg. "Again, it'll get tighter as it dries and you'll experience itching in the days to come. Try not to scratch it, you could break open the lesions before they heal, and perhaps cause an infection."

"I'll try my best not to." Bryce watched as the nurse finished up.

"There, all done. It should be completely set in four or five hours. The good thing is that you'll be able to leave here tomorrow. Make certain you request a cast sleeve before you check out."

"What's that?"

"It's like a rubber pant leg that goes over the cast to keep it dry, so you can shower, bath, whatever." She pushed the table back, scribbled something in his chart, and exited. Bryce looked at the bright white cast and sighed in relief. He couldn't wait to return to Leroy Lake.

Roberto Robertar leaned back in his high back leather chair. He'd been waiting on an important call that he had expected to get an hour earlier. "What the hell is the hold up?" he muttered as he stood and walked over to the office window. The only thing he hated more than having to wait, were people who stood in his way. People like Bryce Ellwood, Hector Foxeagle, and Cameron Kane. People like that, he had no use for. In his opinion, all three of them should be fitted with cement boots and dumped in the nearest swamp. They had cost his company hundreds of thousands of dollars already. If he didn't get the go ahead for the development in the Purgatorys because of their determination to prevent it, his company would ultimately be facing bankruptcy. Staring out the office window, he cursed their antagonistic views.

At Leroy Lake, Hayden was trying to log on to Bryce's computer. Bryce gave him the password, but damn if he could remember it. All he wanted to do was send an email to Colleen, and have her contact the Forestry Service in regard to the grizzly bear he shot. Unable to do so, he stood and exited the tent. His only option was to stay alert and clear of the carcass. It would be attracting more unwanted and hungry visitors, as time went by. Once Bryce returned, he could then report the incident. There was nothing he knew, that he could do to the carcass. That would be up to the Forestry Service and their biologists. Likely they'd fly in and remove it for testing, or torch it where it lay.

Hayden sat down at his makeshift table and looked out across the lake. He contemplated going fishing, but decided against it. In fact, there wasn't much he could do. To leave the camp unattended for any length of time whilst a dead bear lay near was out of the question. Staying close to the tent would at least give him a chance to scare off any intruders. It might also cause another unwanted encounter with another bear, or a number of other carnivorous scavengers. *There's two sides to every coin,* he thought as he averted his eyes toward the carcass, which from where he sat, he could faintly make out.

He looked over to Redeemer who lay near the woodpile, lulled by the warm morning. "It's going to get warm today, cub. Maybe later we'll go for a short stroll along the shore. Won't be fishing today. We're going to have to come up with an alternative activity. I think I'm going to try out that shower." Hayden stood from the table, retrieved a towel from the outside line, and headed for the shower. Redeemer yawned, rolled over onto his back, and stared into space as though he was quite bored. Hayden smiled as he passed him by.

At the Land development office of Robertar & Robertar, Roberto was sipping on his second cup of cappuccino. He finally received the phone call he'd been waiting for and all it did was make his day worse. At the advice of an unnamed BC backbencher, his agenda in regard to the Purgatory land development was put on hold. A three-week ban on his men doing any type of excavating, surveying and or development whatsoever, had been supported by Legislation. Robertar & Robertar would definitely suffer from this, yet, another attempt to slow any progress they may have had by now. It ruffled his feathers some, but he knew the laws, and he'd have to accommodate them, or face a ten-million-dollar fine.

Rising from his desk, Roberto pulled out a file from the cabinet, stuffing it into his briefcase. He locked up the area office then headed for the airport. He half expected the current outcome. With the three-week ban now in place, he decided to return to the main office in Edmonton, Alberta. There were other projects being developed, although none were as extensive or profitable, as what the Purgatory development could be. For the next three weeks he would concentrate his efforts on those, and at the same time do some enquiring on Bryce, Hector and Cam, three opposing forces that he knew in time could and would cause him grief.

Bryce, because of who he was and his expertise, not to mention his journalistic connections to hundreds of magazines, newspapers and the like, was a formidable opponent, and likely the most dangerous to the entire empire of Robertar & Robertar. Hector, because he was an elder of the Ktunaxa people, and was not without great influence, and last but not least, Cameron Kane, for declining the contract Roberto offered him, were all in Roberto's little black book. All three would witness the power of wealth and political influence, if they didn't step down. That was all Roberto thought about as he waited for his private plane to land, so that he could be whisked off to Alberta.

Nick, Roberto's pilot, finally landed. Nick was a scowling old man, who had lost his privilege to fly into the bush country years earlier, and was now allowed to land only on tarmac. Roberto walked the short distance to where he waited. "Afternoon, Roberto. Next time give me more than a two-hour warning, would ya? Had to put off a few other things I had planned."

"Come on, Nick, you're getting paid and likely a lot more than you're worth."

"Shit on you, Roberto. Are you all buckled in?" Nick looked over to Roberto.

"Give me a damn minute. What's your rush?"

"If we don't get a move on, we aren't going to be leaving here until first light. You keep forgetting about the regulations on my pilot endorsement." Nick laughed. He was only joking of course.

"What? I've been gone a couple of weeks and you went and got yourself another violation?"

"Shit, I guess you wouldn't know anything about it. We haven't spoken in a while. I'm not supposed to be within ten feet of a flying apparatus of any kind after dusk," Nick responded as he led Roberto on.

"You got to be kidding me? Are you for real?"

"Damn straight, so hurry the hell up." Nick brushed his thinning salt and pepper hair up into his hat and wiped his brow. His deep grey eyes averted to the plane's instruments and dials. "Look at that, says we're overweight," Nick joked as he pointed at an instrument that meant nothing to Roberto. "Did you put on some extra pounds, Roberto?"

"Sure cocky today, Nick. How about getting them propellers propelling and get me to Edmonton?"

"Finally buckled in then?" Nick looked over to his passenger making certain Roberto was properly seated and buckled. "All right then, off we get." Three minutes later they were taxying down the tarmac picking up speed as they went, and finally taking to the skies. An hour and a half of bad jokes ensued, and by 3:00 p.m., Roberto was sitting in his hot tub back home, expecting a phone call from his son.

His inconceivably large ranch-style house, south east of Edmonton, was an architect's dream come true. He'd paid in excess of three hundred thousand for its design, and at least twice that much to have it built. A five-year widower, Roberto enjoyed nothing more than dazzling young woman with his money and power. He was a pleasure seeker of sorts, and if the house could speak, it could tell plenty of stories. His wife, Carla, had been killed in a car accident at the young age of thirty-nine.

He'd married her when she was seventeen and he was twenty-one. Some of the women he'd entertained since his wife's untimely death, were not much older than his son, Roberto Jr, who was currently studying law on the west-coast. At age twenty-two, he was at the top of his classes at the University of Victoria, UVIC for short. He was a lot like his father. JR. had three things going for him: looks, wealth, and intelligence. He kept his face cleanly shaved, and his black hair docked short. Athletic as he was, and standing at six-foot and 200 pounds Jr. could be an intimidating presence. He wore a diamond-studded earring in his left ear that had been given to him by his mother. His eyes, much like his mother's, were dark blue, but aside from the eyes, JR. was his father's progeny.

The phone call Roberto was expecting from his son as he soaked in the hot tub; was of no dire importance. He'd called him earlier, but JR. wasn't answering the phone or wasn't kicking around, Roberto left a message telling JR. that he was back in Edmonton and would be there for the next couple of weeks, and to call him back when he had a minute. Roberto reached for his glass of Wild Turkey bourbon and took a long swallow. The hot water felt good as the jets massaged his aching back and neck, helping relieve the stress he'd been under. Taking another swallow of bourbon, he set the now empty glass down and picked up his cell phone, deciding that he was in the mood for a little female companionship. He dialled the West End Escort Agency. As a five-year customer, all he ever had to do was tell them who he was. His order was always clean, in good spirits, and healthy, varying in age from nineteen and up. This time around he wanted something different and asked that two girls came instead of one.

The call done, he rose from the hot tub, dried himself and dressed then headed to the game room where he put music on. Stepping behind the black and blue leather wet bar, he grabbed another bottle of Wild Turkey, cracked it open, added ice to his tumbler, filling the glass once more. At 8:00 p.m. his doorbell rang, and a well-deserved night of booze, sex, take out, and partying, ensued. At forty-eight Roberto didn't look a day over forty, and was in as good of shape as he had been in his late thirties. Thank God for his healthy sex drive, he didn't even need the little blue pill.

That evening back at Leroy Lake, Hayden was sitting at the fire, the .308 rifle leaning against a log an arm's length away. It was the furthest he'd been from the tent all day, and the nearest to where the grizzly bear carcass laid. Luckily, there hadn't been any unwanted guests, and Hayden was hoping it'd stay that way. He had a can of beans hanging from the spit by a wire, and sausage frying in a pan. There was no way he wanted to have to give it up because of an interloper.

Redeemer, as usual, lay near, but not near enough that Hayden could reach out and touch him. Averting his eyes to the cub, he shook his head. "When are you going to lighten up cub? I'm not going to hurt you, I'd have thought by now that you'd have clued into that." He waved his hand through the air, "Ah, it doesn't matter. I guess you have your reasons." Rolling the sausage around in the pan, puffs of scented smoke enveloped him, causing his mouth to water. Noting that the beans were done, he removed them from the flame, sat the can on a rock, and waited for them to cool before he dug in.

The sausage was finished as he put the last mouthful of beans into his mouth. Sharing those with Redeemer once they too cooled, he added one more stick to the fire, deciding to relax around its orange flames a while longer. It was a calm night, and except for the wind, which on occasion tousled his hair, the night was still and quiet. The crackling of his fire was the most audible sound.

For a moment he lost himself as he conjured up memories of his past. His time in the Russian Rebel Army, and his defection from both his home in Poski, and the country it was in, flooded his mind. Although seven years had come and gone since, the memories were real and as vivid as if it had all taken place only days earlier. The stinging sensation of smoke in his eyes brought him back to the here and now.

Standing, he stepped away from the fire, noting the cause of the smoke to be the frying pan, which he'd neglected to remove from the flames. All that was left from the fat that was in it, was a solid composition of charcoal. Using a stick he pushed it off the flames. "That was a dumb thing to forget, wasn't it?" he spoke loud enough for Redeemer to hear, but not loud enough to disturb the peaceful silence.

An hour later, as the evening sky darkened, he kicked dirt onto the fire, grabbed the .308 and walked back to the tent. Sitting at the makeshift table, he lit a Colt cigar, took a long pull, coughed then butted it out. Putting his feet up he looked to the evening sky, watching as the first stars began to shine. He was startled moments later when he heard the cries of Redeemer, getting to his feet he looked in the direction that he heard the cries. Hearing Redeemer approach at a full run, he loaded the .308 and quickly shouldered it, ready to fire at any sign of danger.

The cub was twenty yards away when Hayden got

scent of why he was running. An encounter with a skunk obviously frightened the cub. Hayden lowered the rifle, as Redeemer scooted by, up wind of him no less, only to stop a short distance away and roll in the grass. "Whew, got you good, didn't he? It's making my eyes water. Can't imagine what it's doing to yours."

Before Hayden had a chance to get out of the way a family of skunks, a mother and her three offspring were in fast pursuit of the bear cub. He stood steadfast as they slowed down, looked at him then scurried on past straight for Redeemer. The cub though, saw his foe and he high tailed it in the opposite direction, circled around and approached the tent from the east, losing the family of skunk as he did. "Well done cub. I'm afraid though that you still stink to high heaven." Hayden chuckled. "Likely going to stick to you for quite some time too. I can say this much, I certainly don't envy what Bryce is going to be up against once he gets back. There's no way you'll be smelling like a bear by then."

Redeemer was already used to the smell and it no longer bothered him. Hayden on the other hand was plagued by the stink. Hoping to get away from the scent, he decided to head inside and hit the sack. For one reason or another, he felt drained. Retrieving the .308 and glancing around one last time, he bid good night to Redeemer and entered the tent. Leaning the rifle against the tent wall, he slipped out of his boots, rolled out his sleeping bag on Bryce's cot, climbed in and closed his eyes. The powerful scent of skunk roused him from his sleep on more than one occasion, but was soon forgotten as his tiredness overcame him.

Chapter 21

Roberto rolled over in the big four-post king size bed. The two women from the night before lay beside him, their clothes strewn across the bedroom floor. *That was a hell of a good time,* he thought as he stood. Although somewhat hung over, Roberto felt good. He couldn't say the same about the two women. Deciding to let them sleep a while longer, he entered the master bedroom's bathroom, rinsed his mouth, and turned on the shower. The water, hot as it were, felt good as it caressed him.

By 10:00 a.m., the two escorts rose; he paid them and they left. They exchanged no goodbyes, names or otherwise. He knew them only as Quin and Tara. They addressed him as Mr. R., the man with *money.* Roberto watched the security monitor as they pulled out of his driveway, once at the gate he buzzed it open then it closed.

Turning, he walked into his gourmet stainless steel kitchen and poured a cup of cappuccino. Not able to locate the nutmeg or cinnamon he didn't bother; instead he topped the cup with extra whipped cream. Bringing the hot cup to his mouth he took a swallow, licking the whipped cream from his top lip, he decided since he'd be back for the next few weeks, he'd contact his housemaid and have her return bright and early the following day. Since being away, she came only once a week to dust and vacuum. Now though, he needed her every day. Reaching for his cordless phone, he dialled her number. "Good morning Mrs. Macastov. This is Roberto."

"Roberto, good to hear your voice. You back for now?" she asked in a Russian accent.

"Am so, about three weeks. Then I have to head back to the Kootenay office. Are you available for the next couple weeks?"

"For you, Roberto, of course. Shall I come now?"

"Nope. Tomorrow, bright and early."

"That is Friday. Yes, I be there."

"Excellent. All right, I'll see you then." Roberto hung up the phone. He kept Bobbini Macastov on the payroll because she was good at what she did. She was his grocer, housecleaner, mail gatherer, errand runner, and when needed she cooked for him. She also worked side by side with her daughter, twenty-seven or twenty-eight year old Nadine. Roberto liked looking at her. Most men would, her hair grew to the small of her back and was light brown in colour. She had beautiful hazel eyes, which at times appeared to be dark green.

Beautiful she was, full-breasted, athletic, intelligent, she stood five foot seven. Roberto had deep-seated feelings for her. Perhaps it was lust, but whatever it was, Nadine always caused him to have butterflies. She reminded him of his late wife Carla, back in the day when she too was foxy as hell.

Finishing the last of his cappuccino, he set the cup down and walked back to the bedroom, throwing the satin sheets into the hamper and fitting the bed with clean sheets and pillowcases, Roberto opened the big French door that led out to the master bedroom balcony, two stories up. Looking out across the Alberta landscape, he drew in a deep breath at the view he had of all the coulees stretched out as far as his eye could see. The front of his residence as well as the two sides, were skirted with large cedars and aspen. A carpet of imported Kentucky blue grass, grew thick and plush to the tree line. The back, where he stood, was open with only a few shrubs and wild rose bushes. Directly below him was the game room. From it, he could step onto a large concrete patio that boasted of an outdoor heated swimming pool, natural gas barbecue and a bocce ball course. He'd had the yard landscaped for the view, both when sipping cocktails at the poolside, or drinking bourbon on the master bedroom balcony. Each of the rooms on the second floor had a private balcony, all differing in size and shape, and all looking out over the plains.

The first floor was as grand as the second, boasting of a four car indoor garage, game room, home theatre room, library and den, home office suite, dining room, hot-tub, sauna, gourmet kitchen with a built in cooler and stainless steel appliances. Three larger than necessary bathrooms were also on the first floor.

Twelve years ago when the house was first built, it was the perfect size or so it seemed back then, with JR. growing and the countless friends he had, not to mention the many dinner, cocktail, and company parties Carla liked to throw. Now with only him residing there, it was larger than life. Over the years, he thought about selling it, and moving into his three-bedroom condominium on the West Coast. However, JR. had taken up that residence, so Roberto held off selling the house in hopes that one day he could give it to JR. perhaps as a wedding gift if the kid ever decided to marry. It was bought and paid for, not a thing owing on it. Roberto continued his gaze across the coulees as he reminisced.

Eight hours away by land in the New Kootenay General, Bryce was sitting in the hospital lobby waiting for his ride to the Kootenay Forestry landing strip where Cam was going to meet him to take him back into the high country and Leroy Lake. He was desperate to get back to it. He hated hospitals; he hated the smell, the food, everything. Finally seeing his cab arrive, he rose from his chair, and exited into the fresh air of May. Leaning his crutches against the cab he opened the back door and crawled in struggling with the crutches as he did. Settled, he greeted the cabdriver, "Morning, to the Forestry Station, please."

"You all right back there?" the driver asked.

"Yep, am now." he wiggled in the seat and buckled up. Minutes later he paid his fare and entered the Forestry Station. There were only two people on duty and they greeted him.

"Morning, Bryce, we got word that Cam should be landing in the next ten minutes. Want a coffee?"

"Sure. Thanks, Neil." Neil turned and walked into the Conservationists Officer's lounge.

"Heading back to Leroy Lake?"

"Yeah. I have tons of work to do up there still. How have things been going here, Brenda?"

"Pretty good. Things aren't as tense as they are when Jackson is around," she half chuckled. "The party will be ending soon enough, I guess. He's due back early next week."

143

Bryce smiled and nodded, "Hey all good things come to an end sooner or later," he responded to her as Neil returned with his coffee.

"Here you go." Neil handed him the cup of steaming coffee, "freshly brewed, at 7:00 this morning," he joked.

"Anything is better than the coffee back at the Kootenay General." Bryce gently blew the hot coffee then took a drink. "Yep, way better," he added, as he set it on the counter. The three acquaintances conversed for a few minutes until they heard Cam's twin-engine bush plane circle. Bryce finished the coffee, bid Brenda and Neil good bye and met Cam's plane as it slowly came to a halt on the runway. "Good morning, Cam." Bryce said as he opened the door.

"Right back at you. Need a hand getting in?"

"Nah, I can manage. You can take these though." He handed the crutches to Cam.

"No problem." Cam strapped them in behind his seat.

Bryce struggled for a minute until finally crawling in. "There all set," he said, buckling himself in. Cam double-checked making sure Bryce was secure.

"Comfortable?"

"Likely as comfortable as I can get."

"All right then, let's get." The plane left the tarmac at 11:45 a.m. and by 12:00 p.m. Leroy Lake came into view. "There it is. All looks to still be standing," Cam said as he circled. Hayden by now was standing at the shore waiting for the plane to land. Finally after another circle around the lake, it landed on the smooth water and glided to shore. Bryce was the first to open his door. Hayden waded into the water and helped him out.

"Afternoon, Bryce, Cam. How was the flight."

"Good. How have things been here?" Bryce questioned as he waited for Cam to hand him his crutches.

"Got some good fishing in. There is more, but we'll get to that. Are you going to stay for a coffee, Cam?" Hayden asked.

"I suppose. I haven't got anything scheduled." Cam handed the crutches off to Bryce, who hobbled to the shore keeping his leg out of the water as best as he could.

"Good. Come along then," Hayden responded as he met Bryce on the shore. Moments later the three of them walked the distance back to the tent and the pot of coffee.

Bryce noticed the disarray. "What the heck happened here?" he questioned as he looked around.

"A grizzly bear happened here. Had his eye on the cub for dinner. I scared it off then the brazen bastard circled around and charged me. Its carcass is over yonder," Hayden responded as he pointed.

Looking in the direction Hayden was pointing, Bryce and Cam could see the mound of fur fifty or so yards away. "Damn," Bryce said as he looked on, scratching his head. "Have you had a chance to report it?"

"Nope, forgot that password of yours."

Bryce snickered, "It was BRYCE."

Hayden looked at him and shook his head, "Shit, that's right. Can't believe I couldn't remember that. Stupid me," Hayden chuckled as he realised how easy a password it was.

At the realisation that he too had done something stupid, Bryce lowered his own head and shook it. "Never mind that. Stupid me forgot to grab another cell phone."

Cam was sipping coffee, listening to their conversation and when Bryce finished that sentence, he started to chuckle. What he was hearing came straight from the funny pages. "Man, you two are a great pair. One can't remember a simple five-letter password, the other can't think of nothing more than getting back to the mountains, forgetting one of the most convenient ways to communicate, a frigging cell phone."

"Yeah, yeah. Shut up. You got issues there too."

"Like hell I do. I would never have forgotten a cell phone knowing it might save my live." The trio chuckled as they argued all in good fun, jabbing one another.

"Ah, it doesn't matter. I'm not going to be able to wander too far from camp for the next three weeks anyway. As long as my laptop doesn't screw up, I have all the communications I need to the outside world. If I decide, I can grab one when the cast comes off. Which reminds me, are you going to be available to fly me out then?"

"In three weeks eh?" Cam thought for a minute, "Yeah, I suppose. Since you haven't got a cell phone," he jabbed once more. "I'll give you my email address. Email me a day or two beforehand."

"All right. I'll do that."

Cam looked at his watch, "Getting on to 1:00 p.m. I best take to the skies." He swallowed what was left of his coffee. "If you want you can use my cell phone to report the dead bear," Cam said as he looked at Hayden.

"Sure, thanks." Hayden rose from the table and took Cam's cell phone from his hand. "You guys want to take a short walk?" Hayden gestured toward the bear. "I'll be able to describe the bear's condition and size if I'm up near it."

"Good idea, sure thing. Come on, let's go." Bryce gestured to Cam as Hayden began walking the distance. The three of them gathered around the bear, Bryce and Cam both were in awe at the bear's mass. "He's got to be near nine hundred pounds, I'd say." Bryce speculated as he looked down at the bear. "It's an old fellow. Probably would've been his last year anyway," he commented as he used the bottom of a crutch to push up the big bear's top lip. "I can tell that by the condition of his teeth, broken, tarnished and a few missing," Bryce explained to Cam. There was no point in explaining it to Hayden; he already knew.

Hayden, on the phone with Neil back at the Forestry Station, explained the situation, and was told that they'd be by to gather the corpse in a day or two; as soon as the cargo helicopter had been serviced. "All right, I might not be here, but you know how to get in touch with me," Hayden responded.

"Good enough, Hayden. Thanks for reporting it."

"Yep, talk to you later, Neil." Hayden shut the phone off and handed it back to Cam. "Thanks."

"No problem." Cam folded the phone up and tucked it back in its case.

"Neil said they'd be by in a day or two to gather the carcass."

146

"Hope it doesn't get to blustering out. It's going to start to rot anytime now. They'll need take it to the lab and run tests on it, to prove it didn't have rabies." Bryce shook his head knowing how rare that was. "They'll go the extra mile to check it for other possibilities too then run a DNA test on it to make sure it's one of the ones already on record from this area. Could be he's a straggler." He inhaled deeply. "I guess that's it then. Nothing more we can do, might as well head back to camp."

Turning, the three of them made their way back to the tent. At 1:30 p.m., Cam finally took to the skies and headed east. Bryce and Hayden watched as the plane became distant and the droning sound of the twin engine faded. "Well hop-a-long, looks like it's you and I, and that cub of yours." Hayden looked around. "Come to think about it, I haven't seen hide or tail of him since you landed."

"Yeah, he does that. Doesn't like the sound. He'll be back now that the plane is gone," Bryce remarked.

"Rayne showed up the day after Cam airlifted you out of here. She was concerned about you, buddy." Hayden smiled. "I'm pretty sure she has a thing for you," he joked.

"There might be some truth to that," Bryce agreed as he smiled back.

"You mean, she and you…" Hayden started, raising an eyebrow. "You and her had a thing?"

"Not a '*thing*', but certainly shared a few intimate moments." That was all Bryce wanted say about it.

Hayden chuckled. "No need to say more."

"Good," Bryce said as a wryly smile crossed his face. "How about some more coffee, Hayden?"

"Indeed." Hayden pulled out the package of Colts in his pocket and offered one to Bryce.

"When did you take up smoking this cat gut?" Bryce questioned as he took Hayden up on the offer. He too enjoyed the odd cigar.

"Not sure when. One day I realised I was smoking them." Hayden lit a match and held the flame for Bryce.

Taking in a deep lung full, Bryce looked toward the

lake. "Been a while since I inhaled one of these. Taste mighty fine, feels good going down too."

"I figure that's my problem as well. Taste and feeling, the same things we crave and get from our woman," Hayden jabbed.

Bryce chuckled as he felt his cheeks blush, "Ain't that the truth." For the remainder of the day, the two of them conversed, talking about everything and nothing at all. The stink of a skunk wafted in the breeze mildly at first, and then overpowering as Redeemer finally showed.

"Also, forgot to mention your little friend had a run in with a skunk." Hayden chuckled. Redeemer stopped a short distance away, rose on his hind legs, and looked toward the camp where the two men were sitting, realising by both sight and scent that Bryce was back, he dropped to all fours and excitedly ran forward.

He stood as the cub approached. "Hey little buddy," he cooed as Redeemer ran into him, almost toppling him over. "Whoa there bud, can't be doing that to me. Not yet at least. How have you been?" he questioned, stretching out his arm and scratching him behind the ear.

Hayden looked on, "That's something, he won't come close to me. He doesn't seem to like me a whole bunch."

"Ah, he's a bit coy around strangers. He hasn't been formerly introduced to you." Bryce looked at the cub. "Redeemer, that's Hayden, a friend of mine. Hayden this here is Redeemer. Come on over and let him take a sniff of your hand." Bryce gestured.

Hayden stood, walked a few steps then crouched and reached out his hand. At first, the cub backed away, but after some coaxing from Bryce, he finally sniffed Hayden's hand, and at that instant, a new friendship was developed. The bear's warm breath tickled the back of Hayden's hand, causing the hair on his neck to stand. "See cub, like I've always said, I won't hurt you. Took some coaxing from Bryce, for you to realise that, eh?" Hayden smiled as he scratched Redeemer under his chin.

That evening back in Edmonton, Roberto Robertar was

lighting his barbecue when the phone rang. It was JR, the call display told him that. "Well, it's about time you called your old man. How is it going, JR., are they keeping you busy."

"Hey Dad. Yeah they are. So, you're back in Edmonton eh?"

"Yep, been another delay in the Purgatory development."

"That sucks. How long a delay this time?" JR. asked with some concern, but little interest. If he had it his way, he'd be one of those who opposed the project. However, he was a Robertar and that's what Robertar's did. *They were land developers.* Their family name was the signature on countless subdivisions, ski resorts, refineries, even entire city blocks. JR's grandfather had been a developer, his three uncles were developers, even his eleven cousins, all of them, worked in the industry. JR. though, hadn't the same desire. In fact, it was a family joke that he'd be the first Robertar not to be a developer. There was more truth to that than any of them, except JR., wanted to admit.

"Ah, a three week delay is all. No big deal; how have things been going at University?"

"Doing finals now. A little bit stressful, but I'll do okay. Got this semester in the bag."

"Love your attitude, JR. You sound confident. That's a good thing. Don't ever let the man bring you down." Roberto chuckled.

"I'd never let that happen."

"Good. Seeing anyone yet?" Roberto questioned, he always questioned that.

"How come you're always in such a rush to marry me off?" JR. humorously questioned. "I am seeing someone; in fact, she's living with me."

"Good for you. It's about time."

"Shut up."

"What's her name?"

"Parker."

Roberto snickered, "What kind of name is Parker?"

"Want to ask her, she's sitting right here."

"No, no that's okay. What's her last name?"

"Mackenzie."

"An Irish?" Roberto asked as though he were stirred.

"Nope, a Canadian, Dad."

"Parker Mackenzie, eh? I guess it does have a neat ring to it. I still say she's an Irish," Roberto joked. "Ah, regardless, I'm happy for you, son. When do I get to meet her?"

"Actually we were thinking on flying to Edmonton after this semester. The last day of finals is Tuesday, May 18th. It would likely be the 20th when we head that way if we decide to come."

"That would be terrific, I'll still be kicking around here. I'll take you both out and we'll paint the city. I'm sure the three of us could find some kind trouble to get into."

"Yeah, that'd be cool. Anyway, Dad, I got to get going. I have a few papers to look at and chapters to read for tomorrows test."

"All right, JR. If you need anything, let me know."

"I will, Dad."

"Hope to see you on the 20th. I still say she's Irish." Roberto snickered as he hung up the phone. He was beaming with pride and smiling from ear to ear. JR. was turning into a younger version of himself, witty, fearless, confident and ready to take on the world. Whether or not he followed in his footsteps, he'd always be proud of JR., whatever path he chose.

By 11:00 p.m., Alberta time, Roberto was settling in for the night. With a book in his hand and soft music playing, he crawled beneath the clean satin sheets on his king size bed.

Back at Leroy Lake, Bryce and Hayden were doing the same. It had been a long day all around. After rolling out a bed on the tent floor, it took Hayden less than five minutes to fall asleep. Bryce on the other hand, wrestled with it, the cot it seemed was too narrow. Finally rolling up some blankets and propping up his leg, he found a tolerable position. In minutes, he too drifted into sleep.

Chapter 22

At 6:00 a.m., Roberto heard the front door open and the voices of Bobbini Macastov and her daughter Nadine. Looking over to the radio alarm clock, he shook his head. *Couldn't they have come a little later,* he thought, putting a pillow over his head. It didn't take long before the sound of the built in vacuum started up. It whined as one of them vacuumed. Roberto decided to rise, shower and head on downstairs.

"Morning, Bobbini."

"Good morning, Roberto, Nadine has coffee ready."

"Great, I could use some." Roberto walked into the kitchen and poured a cup of the fresh brew. Nadine was in the walk-in pantry taking inventory. "Good morning, Nadine, the coffee is great." He brought the cup to his lips and took a sip, his eyes averted to Nadine.

"Good morning back," she responded, looking over her shoulder. "You need some grub, the pantry is fairly empty. Shall I pick some up for you today?"

"Certainly, Nadine. Let me get my wallet and I'll give you my credit card." Roberto set the coffee down and headed for his bedroom to retrieve his wallet. *God she's beautiful,* he thought of Nadine as he skipped up the stairs. *How I'd like a romp with her.* By the time he returned with his wallet, Nadine had taken from the pantry all the expired this that and the other thing, setting them on the counter. "Wow, that's a lot of expired food."

"Only imperishable items stay good. Everything else eventually expires." Nadine continued cleaning the pantry, and Roberto continued staring at her.

"Here is my card, Nadine." He handed her the card.

"Is there anything special you'd like?"

"Nah, same old same old, I guess."

"Very well. Once I'm finished up here, I'll see how far along my mother has got. If she doesn't need me for an hour or so, I'll go and pick the things up you need." Nadine turned back into the pantry.

"Sure." Roberto rose the coffee cup to his lips and took another swallow. According to the clock on the wall it was past 7:00 a.m. *What can I get done today,* he thought as he took another sip of coffee, his eyes still locked on the beautiful woman in the pantry. He was twenty years her senior, but boy was she appetising. How he wished he were a few years younger, he'd be putting moves on her then.

The thing was, Nadine had a crush on him as well. He was athletic, funny, handsome, and rich. All the thing's women of the twenty-first century wanted in a man. She watched over the years how he looked at her, and always wondered why he hadn't put any moves on her. The only thing she could think was that he wasn't interested in a lowly housecleaner. She couldn't have been more wrong.

Roberto swallowed the last of his coffee and filled the cup once more. "I'll be in the library, Nadine, if there's anything you or your mother need, let me know."

"Thanks." Nadine smiled as she watched him exit the kitchen.

Bryce and Hayden were sitting outside, it was 6:30 a.m., BC time, and the pallid sun stood out from the clear sky, noticeable but not very warm. "Cool one this morning, eh?" Hayden handed Bryce a cup of coffee.

"It'll warm up soon enough. Thanks for the Java," he added as he took the cup of hot brew and nodded.

"Yeah, a couple more weeks and she'll warm up. You got that right." Hayden poured himself a cup of coffee.

"Wonder where that smelly bear cub got to. Haven't seen him yet this morning." Bryce looked around, finally spotting Redeemer near the porta-potty. "Hey, Redeemer, what's going on over there." Whatever it was, Redeemer was amused by it. Bryce shrugged. "Want to go for a short walk? See what that cub is up to?"

"Might as well, couldn't hurt." They rose from the make-shift table. Bryce had some trouble standing for a brief moment. "You all right? Let me give you a hand?" Hayden grabbed Bryce by the shoulder. "Easy does it, buddy," he said as he guided Bryce to the standing position.

"Thanks, Hayden." Bryce snuggled the crutches into his armpits. "There, all set," he commented as he turned and the two made their way over to Redeemer. Unknown to them for the time being, the cub had found himself a little plaything. Being that he had already been sprayed by it countless times, he was used to both the smell and eye irritation the skunk befouled him with. Taking note that Bryce was coming near, he rose, letting the skunk out of his grasp. Instinctively it sprayed in the direction of the oncoming intruders. "It's a skunk!" Bryce said as he halted, holding his breath.

"No kidding, come on let's get the hell out of here!" Hayden responded, as the two turned and made some distance. Redeemer of course followed and following him was his new friend. Neither Bryce nor Hayden could avoid the skunk's second attack. Both were sprayed. Screaming in revolt, Bryce stumbled and fell to the ground, gasping for air. Hayden stopped and turned around, helping Bryce to his feet. The skunk, satisfied with its latest assault, darted toward the undergrowth, and out of sight. "It's gone, buddy, it's gone. For such little vermin they sure throw a punch," Hayden relayed as he watched it disappear.

The two could do nothing but laugh at their misfortune. Laughing harder when they took note of Redeemer, who was looking on as though the two of them were crazy. "That had to have looked funny. There you were, with crutches trying to run, and me, I'm long gone leaving you in the dust," Hayden inhaled deeply as he tried to stop laughing, "then I notice you'd fallen, turned my ass around and run all the way back. While that damn cub looks on as though I've gone mad." The two continued to laugh.

Catching his breath, Bryce spoke, "Don't ask me how we're ever going to get the smell washed off. I don't have enough cans of tomatoes, that's for sure." He shrugged his shoulders. "As for our clothes, we can burn them easy enough. Damn that was funny."

"It was Bryce, it was. I'm glad you didn't break your other leg," Hayden joked. "As for the smell, a couple of showers, some smoke from a campfire and it'll almost be gone. Luckily the clothes took the brunt of it."

"Yeah, but I'm afraid he got my cast good, don't suppose I can change that as easily as clothes. Come on, let's get back to camp, out of these clothes, and burn them." Twenty minutes later, both donning clean clothes, they lit a fire and tossed the dirty ones in. "That'll take care of those. Now about the shower you want to go first?"

"Nah, I figure you took a bigger hit than I, go ahead, I'll clean up later."

"All right then." Bryce hobbled back to the tent for a towel then off to the shower he went. Hayden sat near the morning fire, sipping coffee, a Colt cigar dangled from his mouth. The early morning incident played over in his head and he chuckled to himself. *It could only happen hanging out with Bryce,* he thought. Deciding to go fishing he rose from the fire, grabbed his rod and tackle, and walked the short distance to the shower. He knocked on the door. "Hey, Bryce, I'm going to go cast a line. You going to be okay?"

"Yeah, sure thing. No worries."

"All right. I might take the canoe." Hayden turned and walked to the lake, deciding to cast his line in near the spot where he first fished along the shore. Sitting down he slowly reeled the line in. His fourth cast went a further distance then the others and he reeled it in slow, jigging every now and again. Suddenly the line grew taut, and the fishing reel whined. Adjusting the tension, and giving the rod a few quick jerks he began reeling in.

The fish cleared the water, dove deep then out again. Hayden stood and continued reeling in. The rod bent and he thought it might break. Letting out line he waited for the rod to become straight again then continued reeling. The fish cleared the water for the fifth or sixth time, and he got a glimpse of the shimmer as it once more dove to depths unknown.

For ten minutes, angler and fish battled. Finally becoming the victor, Hayden reeled it to shore. It was then that he felt the eyes upon him. Looking to his left and standing not less than a hundred feet away, was a mother black bear and her two cubs. She stood on her hind legs, looking on as her two cubs frolicked in the water. Hayden's only choice was to toss the big fish toward her as she darted in his direction, in either a full-blown charge or a threatening gesture for him to back away. Whatever it was, he wasted no time turning and walking away. To run would be fruitless, had she been farther away he might have considered it. When he felt safe he stopped and looked back. The bear and her cubs were feasting on the fish, and no longer was she a threatening force. She was content with the fish rather than exerting her energy in chasing after him.

Hayden watched as the bear and her cubs finished then vanished into the forest. He shook his head. It was the second time that a bear took off with his catch, Redeemer being the first. Scratching his whiskered chin, he turned and headed back to camp. A mother bear and her cubs strutting about could cause grief for he or Bryce. At camp he'd be a lot safer. Bryce had been out of the shower for a few minutes when Hayden finally made his way back. "Just saw a mother black and her two cub's," Hayden commented as he set his rod and tackle down, sitting down next to Bryce.

"Excellent. Two cubs you say?"

"Yep."

"You didn't notice if the cubs had any older siblings?" Bryce questioned with curiosity.

"Only saw the two cubs. I'd say they were this year's. Pretty small, both of them."

"How'd the mother look? Was she scrawny?"

"I'd say as scrawny as most bears are at this time of year. She didn't appear to be ravenous by any means. A lot of vegetation in the area, I assume she's been feeding on that. Mind you, she did take a run at me, I figure she wanted me clear of her cubs. To slow her down I tossed her a fish, a big fellow too. Eighteen or so inches long and near half that deep."

"Are you telling me a fish tale, Hayden?" Bryce chuckled.

"Nope. Honest to goodness, that's how big it was." Hayden spread his arms out gesturing the length and breadth of his catch. "There are more out there that size too. I guarantee it. One broke my line the other day."

"Huh, maybe I'll cast a line in after I'm healed a bit. That aside, I'm glad the bears are beginning to show. It'll make for a few interesting weeks while I heal, especially if they're going to be hanging out at the lake. Makes my work a lot more interesting," Bryce said with enthusiasm. "Won't have to hobble around here looking at birds and flora. I guessed I'd glimpse the odd deer, moose, cat and what have you, but never thought about bears down this low. Figured I'd have to hike around some. What you told me is good news."

"I thought you'd like to know. Going to have to be careful though; keep your wits. Three weeks is a long time to be hobbling out here. You might consider asking Jackson to send a replacement until you're walking."

"Never. There's no need for that. I'll be okay, Hayden, don't you worry. There's a lot I can do right here at camp. Won't have to go any further than the lake shore or the bush."

Hayden averted his eyes the distance of the lake and the bush line. *Bryce was right. He'd be okay.* "I suppose you're right. As long as you stay vigilant, having that cub of yours around might cause a tiff with something, like it did with that grizzly. That's what I'd be concerned with. What are you going to do with that animal, anyway? He's going to start growing like weed this summer."

"My intent was to always re-introduce him to the wild, once he was big enough to take care of himself. Lately I've been letting him roam. I try not to interfere with him unless he's in need of something." He looked over to the cub lying beside the woodpile. "A while back I thought about contacting Fences, Cages & Co and have them build a fence around ten or so acres of my property back in Parkview. I decided against that though. Think I'll leave him back here when the time comes." Bryce sighed. "Not sure though, I might make that call. I could let him roam my land for a few years, and then let the fence down one day."

"You're the one that will have to decide upon that. I figure he'd do fine if you left him here. Then again, anything could happen. I know this much, there is a lot of red tape involved in getting a permit for bears. You'll be looking at a cost in legal fees of easily ten maybe fifteen grand."

"Might even be a bit more than that. The cost for me really isn't the issue, the morality of it is."

"Yeah, there's that," Hayden responded as he thought for a moment. "I'll tell you what, if you ever need my backing, financial or otherwise, I'll help you out."

Bryce looked at him quizzically, "What are you saying?"

"I have some bling-bling left from you know what...and I'd be more than happy to help you out."

"Yeah, yeah. I know." Bryce always felt uncomfortable talking about all the money Hayden and two of Hayden's childhood friends, stole from the DEA years earlier while he defected from Russia. His opinion though was much like Hayden's, the DEA and US Government, had confiscated the money from a drug lord, and therefore fair game.

"All right, I won't mention it again. Just keep it in mind," Hayden responded noting Bryce's uneasiness about the subject.

Bryce nodded, "Might take you up on it," he said as he winked. From what he knew of the money Hayden had made off with, it was in the tens of millions, in fact the three of them each walked away with that amount. Unfortunately a death did occur. Hayden's long time childhood friend, Alex was the causality, and only Hayden and Alex's sister, Monique survived. That was all he knew and all he wanted to know. Some things were better left alone. Bryce could not condemn Hayden's shaded past, nor could he condone it. Hayden was Hayden, and he took him for the man he was today. His past meant nothing. Everyone had one of those.

The two sat in the comfort of each other's presence, sipping coffee and reminiscing. Bryce took note of the dark clouds approaching from the north. "By the sight of those clouds we'll be getting a storm."

Hayden followed Bryce's gaze. "Yep. Likely some snow in the higher elevations." Hayden took out the package of Colt cigars from his pocket and offered one to Bryce. "Care for one." Hayden gestured with the package.

"Yeah, if nothing else it'll keep the mosquitoes at bay." He took one and stuck it between his teeth. "Heading back tomorrow, Hayden, or can I coax you to stay another day or two?"

"Depends on what tomorrow brings I guess, but I was thinking about it, yeah. Likely got things to catch up on back at the fort."

"If you decide to stay a day or two longer you'd be more than welcome. There were a few things I wanted to talk to you about, in regard to a protest Rayne's planning for Ottawa."

"Hmmm, interesting. A protest eh?" Hayden chuckled. "Haven't been to one of those in some time."

"That's just it, Hayden, I need you to convince them not to. That kind of press at this stage isn't going to make a difference. What the Coalition needs more than bad press, are donations of money and time. A campaign in that regard will be more successful. There are some things I've discovered about Robertar & Robertar, and if we can prevent them from developing these mountains," Bryce said referring to the Purgatorys, "they'll be dead in the water, tits up, bankrupt."

"Aha, I see. I'm glad it's that way. I wasn't sure if I could be of any help. With a protest, that is. That stuff doesn't shoot through my veins much anymore."

"That's how I feel. I tried to convince them, Hector and Rayne, that to protest would only piss the Government and their agencies off. That type of movement isn't as effective nowadays, as it might have been in the eighties. Today, influence talks and bullshit walks. That's what's going to stop any further plans for a five star ski resort to be permanently etched into the Purgatorys."

"Are you talking about a fund raiser type of thing?"

"Fundraiser's, advertisements, radio, television, whatever else can attract the press, except protests. That's what I'm talking about."

"You've heard of the Conservatory for Environment,

right?"

"Yep, and I know where you're going with that. If we could raise enough money, we could buy a large chunk of this land. At least protect it from any development whatsoever. I've had that thought often. If we could convince Hector and Rayne both that a better offensive move to protect this land is with cash and the pen, we might get somewhere."

"Once I get back to the fort I'll have Colleen do some research on them, you know, the Conservatory for Environment. Find out what has already been done, what can be done, and where we can start. I'd be more than willing to part with some cash, upwards of two or three million, to start it off. As for convincing Rayne and Hector, not sure I can do any better than you. I will try though, rest assured."

"That's all I ask. Can't do any more than that." Then it dawned on Bryce what Hayden said, in regard to the cash amount he'd be willing to donate for the cause. He looked over to Hayden, his eyes big. "Did you say two or three million?" Bryce asked as he swallowed deeply.

"For sure. That's exactly what I said. I figure it's for a good cause. Besides, there's some big fish in that Lake. I'd hate to be unable to fish it again." Hayden chortled with sincerity and assurance.

"Excellent, truly excellent; your generosity will go a long way."

"I have no doubts. It's beautiful up here, serene and ghostly all at the same time." The two averted their eyes to the mountains, the lake, the forests of coniferous trees and rock bluffs, and crags that made up the landscape. The dark menacing clouds to the north were closing in fast. In the distance as they looked on, lightning flashed and snaked across the sky followed by a loud clap of thunder.

"Let's get these blocks of wood and table top beneath the tent awning, or we're going to be soaked." No sooner had Hayden said that than the rain hit. They quickly tossed the tabletop under the awning and rolled the two pieces of wood behind it. "There, that's better," Hayden said as he set it up again. "Can watch now in comfort." Sitting he looked out across the lake. Rain peppered the awning and streams of water boiled down the front of it. The sound was deafening as it pelted down unrelenting and with hostility. "Quite the downpour," Hayden said above the sound.

Bryce nodded, "Yeah, no kidding. Haven't seen it pour like that since I've been up here. The sound is almost maddening," he hollered back. A moment later Redeemer came darting for cover, stinking to high heaven of wet bear and skunk. Hayden and Bryce both wrinkled up their noses. "My god, that's a powerful stench, Redeemer. You got to go and roll in the grass or something."

Redeemer drew closer, brushing his snout against Bryce's arm. Then he turned and headed for his sweater beneath the awning and near the woodpile. There he curled up and watched with them as the rain continued its assault. It took a few minutes, but eventually Bryce and Hayden grew used to the stink Redeemer emanated.

The storm passed Edmonton, Alberta but not without havoc. Roberto Robertar was looking out his library window, watching as the dark clouds expended south westerly. It hit Edmonton hard, cutting the power to most of the city and as far away as Roberto's. He stood with a tumbler of bourbon in his hand. Bobbini and Nadine had already left for the day. Bobbini God bless her, put a chicken on the rotisserie and told him to keep an eye on it, that it would be ready in two hours near 5:00 p.m. However, the distraction of the storm and power being out, caused him to neglect her instructions and he soon forgot. In normal circumstances it wouldn't have mattered as the timer would have shut the appliance off.

Now though, once the power kicked back on, if he didn't shut the oven off manually when he set the clock, the chicken would cook indefinitely until he noticed either the smoke or heard the smoke alarms. The latterly being the most likely as he was now nursing his second bourbon. He hadn't accomplished much that day, but decided that the rest was due.

He did manage to read through a few developing plans in regards to other projects. He called a few friends, set up a meeting for the following Wednesday, May 19, with an Edmonton journalist who had been relentlessly pursuing the development in the Purgatorys and wanted to know more about the recent development freeze, what it meant to the company, how far along they were, how much opposition were they facing, blah, blah, blah. Roberto shook his head as he swallowed the last swig of bourbon.

Making his way to the game room, he carried the empty bottle of bourbon in his left hand, and his empty glass in his right. It was only a quarter full when he grabbed it, and now he was going back for a fresh bottle. He hadn't decided yet whether it would be a bottle of bourbon, Vodka, or something less intimidating, like a good bottle of wine. Standing now behind the bar, he opened the mirrored door and glanced over the bottles of booze. Unable to make up his mind he closed the cabinet door, took a few steps forward and opened the wine cooler, deciding finally upon a bottle of CG's Garden Gold 2002, a worthy vintage in his mind. Opening the bottle he poured a glass and walked back to the library where he sat down in his big easy chair.

The power still hadn't kicked back on yet, and he knew he was in for a wait. It didn't matter though; he had the bottle of wine, and a hand full of cigars sat in a box on the reading table next to the chair. All was well. At 10:00 p.m., all hell broke loose, the smoke alarm went off and the radio buzzed. Roberto sat up and could smell the acrid smoke of something burning, trying to stand in his drunken and confused state, he fell face forward and bounced off the floor.

Finally able to stand, he shook himself off. The alarm and radio buzzed with an abatable nuisance. Stumbling he darted for the library exit and into the lobby. Awake now from the fall, the sound, and the smoke billowing from under the kitchen door, Roberto was brought back to reality, remembering the chicken in the oven. "Stupid me!" he said out loud, as he made his way into the smoke filled room.

Turning the stove off, he switched on the overhead exhaust fan then crossed over to the control panel that shut off the alarm, pushing the flashing red button, sighing with relief when it went silent. "Thank God for that," he muttered as he made his way out. He'd check back in a bit after the smoke had a chance to escape. *That was a close one, Roberto, that was a close one,* he thought as he threw himself down on the lobby couch. He didn't rise again until the following morning, and only when he heard Bobbini's voice.

"Mr. Robertar, what on earth, it's 5:00 a.m. Come on, get up. I'll help you to bed."

"Morning, Bobbini, that's all right I'm okay. I can make my own way there," he said as he slowly sat up and rose. "Oh yeah, I think there was a fire in the kitchen last night." He ran his hand threw his hair as he thought for a moment indeed there had been a fire. It was the chicken, he remembered now. "Actually, that chicken I forgot about it after the power went off."

"You burned my chicken, I especially make for you. You had too many bourbon, and on an empty stomach too I think. Now off to bed with you. Sleep off your stupor, Mr. Roberto. There isn't much Nadine and I need to do today, we'll be out of your hair in an hour or two...burn my chicken," she added as she walked away to face the mess. Roberto climbed the stairs to his room. The empty bed never looked so inviting and he fell upon it half drunk, asleep before he found a pillow.

Chapter 23

While Roberto slept off his hangover, Bryce and Hayden sat under the tent awning. The storm from the past night made all things miserable. Even now, as they sipped their morning coffee's, the rain continued, not as hard or fierce, but constant. Fog hung over Leroy Lake, like a halo it enveloped their surroundings, even the Purgatory Mountains were hidden by the low hanging fog.

A wet and miserable morning it was indeed. Hayden poured himself another coffee and sat back down. "Won't be heading back yet, not until this weather lifts." He took a drink from his cup.

"Likely it'll stay for most of the day. Once the fog clears up, things will get better," Bryce responded, as he too took a swallow from his coffee. "I'm glad it isn't coming down like last night. Could hardly sleep with the constant pitter-patter, sounded like I was inside a drum. How about you, Hayden, how well did you sleep?"

"Sounds as though I slept as well as you." The scent of rotting carrion wafted their way on the breeze. "Smell that?" Hayden questioned. "That dead grizzly is starting to get ripe. Going to attract an array of scavengers in the next while if the Forestry Service doesn't get up here and take it away."

"Yep, you got that right. They won't be flying in today with the weather as it is. It's been what, three days dead?"

"Nope, four. Four days dead and starting to stink." Hayden averted his eyes to the lake. His rod and tackle were calling him. "Since I'm here for at least today. I figure once the rain halts, I'm going to cast in a line. The fish will be in a frenzy then."

Bryce nodded, "Once I get the get-up-and-go, I'm going to try and catch up on my log books and gather any email that might be waiting. After that, I might join you depending on how my leg feels. It doesn't feel so bad now, but a couple of hops, skips and jumps, there'll be a twinge as constant as the rain last night."

"What about the itch, you got the itch yet?" Hayden

questioned as he snickered.

"Damn it, you had to bring that up. Yeah I got it all right; I've been trying to ignore it, until now. Thanks, buddy," Bryce said with sarcasm.

"Ah, no need to thank me. After all, what are friends for?" Turning his head, Hayden chuckled. "Well, if you got the itch, it means it's healing." Hayden drew in a breath, "By the way, how itchy is it? Real itchy, or a little itchy?"

Bryce knew well enough what Hayden was doing, and he chuckled. "You're a jackass, you know that. Change the subject would you?"

Smiling, Hayden scratched his own head then his shoulder. "Yeah, all right."

Bryce watching his antics, began to feel a terrible urge to scratch his leg. "Keep it up, Hayden and my urge to scratch might be to club you with my crutch instead," he joked. The two sat through another pot of coffee, reminiscing and waiting for the fog and weather to lift. By 11:00 a.m., the sun broke through and the fog dissipated. It didn't take long for Hayden to head to the lake, rod in hand. The skies above were clear and blue, the sun a welcoming entity. It was turning out to be a fine day after all.

Bryce made himself comfortable as he booted up his laptop. A memo in his inbox was marked urgent and he clicked it on. It was from Jackson's office and three days old. Bryce read it and smiled. Apparently, the development that Robertar & Robertar were planning for the Purgatorys had been put on hold. A three week ban on any further development, surveying etc, had been passed.

As of May 12, 2004, not even a company truck or any associate of his whatsoever, was allowed in the immediate area. There was also a ten million-dollar fine proposed, if he didn't abide. Obviously, it was that way to prevent Robertar & Robertar from subcontracting any surveying company, land developer, or the like. For three weeks, they'd been in a complete deadlock. Nothing could be done. Although it was only a three-week ban, a preventative action such as that would slow the progress down and at a great monetary loss to the Company.

It made Bryce's day, and he couldn't wipe the smile off his face as he continued reading his other mail most of which was junk. Logging off the World Wide Web, he turned his attention to the paper work and cataloguing he was behind in. Devoting the next hour to catch up, he finally rose from the hard chair and stretched. Noting that it was 1:00 p.m., he ambled outside.

Hayden was down at the lake still fishing, and behind him, hidden somewhat by grass and bramble, Redeemer lay, waiting for a catch. Hayden wasn't having much luck though; the entire time he only got three bites but no trophy. Discouraged, he reeled in his line and made his way back to the tent.

"Where's the fish?" Bryce chortled, as he made the distance back.

"A couple of bites, but no trophy, my friend. Caught up on your paperwork?" Hayden pulled up to the table and sat down.

"Not really, got a cool email though. As of May 12, 2004, legislation passed a three-week ban on Roberto's company doing any work up here. Not even associates of his are allowed in the immediate area." Bryce was smiling as he relayed the information.

"Three weeks for a company like his has got to hurt his pocket book, not to mention piss him off." Hayden poured a coffee, a smirk all his own across his face. "Although I didn't catch any fish, what you said makes my day."

Bryce nodded, "Mine too."

"Whether or not the sly bastard abides, is another story," Hayden added, as he brought the cup of coffee to his mouth and took a drink.

"There's a ten-million-dollar fine if he doesn't. Don't think Roberto would want to risk a loss like that."

"Ten million for a fellow like Roberto is a drop in the bucket, he'll make ten times that and probably more, if he finally gets the go ahead to develop a five-star ski resort up here."

"Hopefully it won't come to that. The opposition isn't as great as it was in 1988, but there is some, and like we talked about last night, if we can get a campaign going to raise funds, we might have a chance of preventing the entire charade."

At 3:00 p.m., Alberta time, Roberto was beginning to stir. The sun glared through the bedroom window, blinding him as he opened his eyes. Hung over and hungry, he made his way to the kitchen and made a sandwich. There were three messages waiting for him on his answering machine and he pushed the button to listen. The first was from Foster Codwell of Codwell, Budaka, & Francois Associates. There had been some new financial developments and they needed to verify a few things.

The second was from JR. He and Parker weren't going to be able to make the trip after all. Roberto felt a tinge of disappointment, but he shrugged, *another time I guess.* There wasn't much he could do. *Maybe I'll surprise them. It'd blow JR's mind if I showed up down there,* he thought as he listened to the third message. It was again, from Foster Codwell, urging Roberto to call. "Yeah, yeah. I'll call when I'm good and ready," he said out loud, as he turned the answering machine off. He knew that if it were financial then it wasn't good. For now, all he wanted was for his head to quit pounding and his hunger pangs to go away.

He made his way to the sauna and turned it on, while it heated up he threw together another sandwich, pouring a glass of buttermilk to coat his sour stomach, swallowing the last of it, he burped, set his cup down and headed for the sauna to sweat what was left of his hangover out.

Removing the towel from around his waist, he added a drop or two of eucalyptus oil to the washtub of water that sat on the fake glowing rocks. It produced billows of steam every three or four minutes and he inhaled deeply. The aromatic scent cleared both his sinuses and his head. He felt better already. Turning he sat down on the cedar bench with his back against the wall. The eucalyptus scented steam made his skin feel cool and refreshed. *Nothing like a sauna to soak out the booze,* he thought as he sat.

An hour later, feeling his usual self, Roberto was sitting in the home theatre room, watching a program on his projection television screen. A bottle of brandy, as well as some cold cuts and crackers he'd thrown together, were within his reach. He was settling into the big house nicely. Away for most of the winter and spring, the house sat dormant. Now though as he settled in, it was looking and feeling more like the home he remembered. *I guess it isn't so bad, being the only one here,* he thought as he poured a brandy.

The ringing sound of the phone sitting on the table next to him, broke the solitude of the moment, and he answered. "Hello."

"Afternoon Roberto, this is Foster. Have you got any of my messages? Been tying to get a hold of you since yesterday."

Roberto looked over to the plate of crackers, "Nope. Just got in less than a half-hour ago," he lied. "What's up?"

"This latest three-week ban is really putting a squeeze on your overhead. One of our investors says if they don't see some kind of progress in a month, they'll fold and pull out."

Roberto exhaled heavily, *great that's all I need to hear,* he thought. "Which investor is that? And what's at stake, Foster?"

"It's Strangehaur & Field, they've invested nearly twenty-three million. Take them out of the picture and the noose around our necks is a lot tighter."

"How tight, exactly? Will Robertar & Robertar be okay without their investment?"

There was a pause at the end of the line as Foster briefly thumbed through a financial statement. "You'd be okay for a time, but if the development falls through, you know what that'll mean. You're nearing a two-month delay as it is, with this new ban. Every day that your guys have to sit idle, you're losing security interest."

"There's really nothing I can do. I have to abide by the rules that legislation lays out."

"I know. I'll see if I can't hold on to Strangehaur & Field. I'd hate to lose their investment. I don't suppose you'd bend the rules a bit and considering sending a subcontractor up there to the Purgatorys to do some surveying? At least then I'd have some kind of data to show those that have invested."

"I've thought about that, but I don't think I could take a ten-million-dollar hit."

"You'd only suffer that if someone clued in. Ten million is a lot less than the hundred or so million riding on this development. Besides, there are a few loopholes in the ban."

"I agree that there are loop holes. Let me sleep on it for a day or two, Foster. Get back to me on Monday or Tuesday. Do me a favour too, Foster, find out for me who that BC backbencher was that got the ban initiated."

"Okay, I can find that out. Shouldn't be a problem. I'll talk to you then in a couple days." Foster hung up the phone. Inhaling deeply, Roberto shook his head. He hated having to play dirty pool, although that's what built up his company, it didn't appeal to him like it used to. He took a long swallow of brandy and emptied the glass. Filling it again, he stood and walked over to the big bay window. Looking out westerly in the direction of the Purgatorys, he sipped his second brandy.

He wanted nothing more than to finally get the go ahead for the development. He knew how much the net profit could be, and it was a lot more than his company ever made. Not only that, it would generate full-time income for numerous people, and for an area as depressed as British Columbia, he would have thought that the people would be a lot more receptive to the ideology of a better economy. *BC is certainly full of hot heads and people who believe in the simplicity of life, rather than economics,* Roberto thought, as he took another swig from the glass of brandy he held in his hand.

There were animal habitats at stake as well, and he knew that. The big picture was in his mind and always had been that the animals wouldn't really be hurt at all. They'd simply move further into the Rocky Mountains and even then not all would do so, a lot would stay behind, and coexist, much as in other resorts all across Canada.

Then there was the spiel about the safety of the area, and the possibility that the entire resort could be wiped out by a looming avalanche or landslide. Again, in his opinion, it was a bunch of hooey and speculation. His own engineers had taken all that into account, and would take preventative measures if needed. That was a given. Yet, here he was faced with a three-week development ban and an opposition that was taking form. Roberto sighed. *Like all things in life, nothing is easy.*

He knew two things with certainty. If the development didn't take place, British Columbia would lose in excess of a billion dollars a year in the tourism industry, and Robertar & Robertar would have to make major cutbacks or face bankruptcy. The outcome, as far as he was concerned, had to go his way. Taking another sip of brandy, Roberto closed the blinds and curtain then and returned to his seat in front of the big projection screen.

Back at Leroy Lake, Bryce and Hayden were roasting sausages over an open flame, and drinking coffee. Their day had been uneventful. The weather had put a damper on things. Even when the sun finally came out everything seemed to have slowed down. Hayden hadn't even caught any fish. The only good thing that came about that day, was the email Bryce received. It was enough to keep their spirits up, even now as the mosquitoes and black flies tried their patience. "That sausage is sure smelling good?" Hayden remarked as he swatted his hand through the air scooting off a swarm of black flies circling his head.

"Pesky aren't they?" Bryce commented referring to the flies and mosquitoes.

"Indeed." Hayden turned his stick with the sausage impaled on it. "It's nature though. They feed the birds and such."

"I suppose. Still, they're a pain in the ass as far as I'm concerned."

"I wouldn't disagree." Hayden turned the stick once more. "Looks like she's done." Removing the stick from the fire, he gently blew the sizzling sausage. "Yep, done as done can be." He brought the hot meat to his mouth and bit a piece off. Savouring the taste, he nodded. "That's good." he commented as he continued eating.

"Everything is always better when cooked on a flame." Bryce removed his own stick from the flame and followed suit. The taste indeed was heavenly. "Don't know what the Mennonites put in it, whatever it is, they sure know how to make sausage." They cooked two more half rings each and reminisced. By 9:00 p.m., finally overwhelmed with the flying insect population, the two turned in.

Chapter 24

A ten-mile hike to Toby Creek that morning awaited Hayden. Up before the sun rose, he and Bryce sat together and drank a coffee. "Figure you're going to be all right, way up here with crutches?" he asked.

"You already know the answer to that, buddy. Of course, I'll be all right. No need for you to worry in that regard."

"Just digging for assurance. Hate to leave you here to only find out later something happened to you." Hayden rose from the table and gathered his rod. Disassembling it, he stuffed it in his pack along with all his other gear.

"What could happen? As long as I stay close to camp, I'll be fine." Bryce was certain of that.

"I suppose so, after all you did manage when the thing was broken," Hayden said as he gestured toward Bryce's cast. "Keep the .308 close, least until the Forestry guys remove the carcass. I hope that'll be sometime today. If not, be wary of what's going to start scavenging it. It's early enough that there are going to be some hungry unwanted visitors, whether that carcass is there or not." Hayden looked toward the lake. "Spring at this altitude has only sprung. If you know what I mean, the carcass will only tantalise instincts." He shouldered his packsack.

"I'll stay vigilant, Hayden, don't you worry. And yes I'll keep the rifle close." Bryce hobbled to his feet and leaning on a crutch, reaching out his hand to shake Hayden's. Nodding, Hayden shook his hand.

"You still have Colleen's email address?"

"Yeah, it's been added to my address book."

"Good. If you need to get me for any reason at all, between now and when they remove that cast, and before you get another cell phone, email me would you?"

"Most definitely. Say hi to Colleen for me, as well as Rayne and Hector. Let them know I'm all right."

"Will do. I might stop back in a couple of months. Until then, I'll see what I can get rolling with the things we

171

talked about. I'll stay in contact with you in regard to any progress."

"Right on," Bryce nodded, waving as Hayden turned and walked north-westerly toward Toby Creek and civilisation. He continued his gaze until Hayden disappeared into the forest and out of sight. Sitting back down, he poured another coffee. *Alone again,* he thought, sighing with both contentment and regret.

Hayden steadily walked for an hour, stopping only to relieve himself or to catch his breath. Keeping to that pace, he managed five miles before the sun was hot. The mild breeze that mixed with the warm air was scantily scented with cedar and pine, and it tousled his hair when he found a place to sit.

Opening his pack, he reached in and pulled out a stick of pepperoni, surprised actually that it still smelled and looked good, although a few days old. He fumbled again inside, coming up with a V8 and a bag of peanuts. *Good enough,* he thought as he snacked on the items. He rested until his Iron Man wristwatch chimed in at 11:00 a.m. Rising, he shouldered the pack, and once more set off.

Finally he could smell smoke from Hector's cabin. "It won't be long now," he said to himself. Ten minutes later he was greeted by Hector, standing on the back porch of the cabin.

"Hayden, it is good to see you. How is the man at the lake whose Indian name shall be known as Bryce, the next time I see him." Hector laughed at his own joke.

"Bryce is fine; he sends his regards. How have you folks been?" he questioned as he nodded his acknowledgement to Rayne, who now stepped outside.

"Rayne and I, we stay good. Come, sit. You must be weary." Hector gestured for him to sit.

"Thank you." Hayden removed his pack, pulled up to the table, and sat down. "Nice walk this morning. Couldn't have asked for better weather, leastwise, compared to that storm the other day. Wasn't that something?"

"It is all good. Better than a dry spring. Could have done without the chill." Hector gazed out across the mountains, "Up high, there will be snow tonight."

"Likely there's some up there already."

"Yes, but more will come. Spring this year is leery; it's afraid to come and dry up the mountain passages, so that this land can be ravished by the money hungry man who wishes to do so."

"You've heard that a three week ban on Robertar doing any excavating, surveying or development of any kind has been dutifully applied, as well as a minimum ten-million-dollar proposed fine, if he doesn't abide, haven't you?" Hayden questioned. Surely the news spread by now via the radio, or television and most definitely in a newspaper.

Hector looked at him, surprised and curious. "Have not heard. It is a good omen, this news you bring. As good as it is or may seem, it means he has only been slowed for a short while. He needs to be halted absolutely, and for good, nothing less, and I would not wish upon him nothing more." Hayden listened intently as Hector spoke. Everything he said was sincere and spoken with great thought.

"Bryce and I the other day were talking, and although neither one of us could condemn the idea of a protest, we did agree there is a better route to do exactly what a protest won't," Hayden grew silent as he looked at their surprised faces, "and that's to get people to listen. I know that probably isn't what either one of you were hoping I was going to say. The reality is a protest in this day and age is more likely to get bad press than good press." Hayden paused as he waited for one of them to respond.

"Are you saying, Hayden, that we should rethink the actions we were all going to take?" Rayne asked with annoyance as though what he'd said was an insult.

"I guess that's what it boils down to. Think about it; a campaign in raising money through awareness and education. The word is that Robertar & Robertar are standing on their last legs and if they lose their bid to proceed, they'll be bankrupt, destroyed, nullified. I personally have already agreed to start the thing off. I figure with both of your help in raising awareness, and perhaps a few live Q&A workshops at schools, colleges, and the like, we could all work together and shut Robertar & Robertar down. As well, we could prevent any other land developer from even considering a second glance at the Purgatorys for years to come."

Hector, who had been leaning forward, now leaned back and crossed his arms. "What is this proposition you introduce? I think I hear again, the white man talking. Children, what can they do? Yes, indeed they are our future, but we need a solution now. You talk about speaking to children. Their influences will be viable only in the future, not today."

"Actually, Hector that would only be a side venture. The main goal at first is to raise money by way of donation, as well as fund raising. The money that's raised we use to go right over Robertar's head, using a secondary Coalition called the Conservatory for Environment. We purchase as much of the land as we can then the land remains as is, wild and free."

Hector looked over to Rayne. He could tell she was in deep contemplation. "The Granddaughter, her voices are speaking to her. I think she thinks your idea needs greater thought. Because my ways seem old to you both, I will let her decide if this new argument has merit." Hector paused as he looked out once more toward the mountains. "Perhaps, your way is the way."

"Yes, Grandfather, Hayden's way will have more impact. Remember the saying Grandfather, 'the pen is mightier than the sword'." Hector however, stubborn as he was, did not respond. All that Rayne said landed on deaf ears. Rayne looked to Hayden and smiled. "I will work on Grandfather. He is old and has a different point of view than most."

"Yeah, I know. No need explaining." Hayden shrugged his shoulders and smiled.

"Now that we're past that. Do you have time for tea and biscuits?" Rayne asked.

"Would love a cup of tea and certainly wouldn't turn down any biscuits."

Rayne rose from the table and entered the cabin.

Hector still motionless, continued his gaze to the mountains. "Sometimes the Granddaughter even thinks like the white man," he muttered as his eyes averted to Hayden. "It is society that teaches her this. The Indian way has been taken from her and from many others as well. I think that your way, the way of the white man, is our only hope. I say that now, because you have said in not so many words that no one would listen to a bunch of Indians. That is honesty. You are right. I see it in my Granddaughter every day."

Hayden listened, wondering how Hector came up with that accusation. As he thought, he realised, Hector was right, feeling remorse and shame as Hector finished. Hayden understood. Society had turned the white man into the person he was today. No one really cared about anyone else. If you were rich, you had no worries. If you were poor, that's all you had. It was a dog-eat-dog world, and it would seem that those with money and influence in today's society, were all who counted. Hayden realised then, that even Canada, the land of freedom and choice, was marred with Capitalism.

"I wasn't trying to be offensive, you have to understand that. What you said about society is undoubtedly true; it is disheartening. It is also what our society has become. It is not nationality, creed, white man, black man, or other. It is the will to change for better, and obviously *for worse*. Mankind has turned soft because of all the change. There was a time we didn't need or even want, half the things that are available for us to consume, like the mountains, timber, heck I could go on and on. The point is you are right about society. We are too far ahead of ourselves to change. Some will try and most will lose." Hayden now averted his eyes to the impressive mountain, wondering if what he'd said made any sense.

"You see things through the eyes of minorities, less privileged and the poor. I am glad that you and I see things the same. For those reasons, I have decided that the Ktunaxa people, and our friends, will follow you in this conquest to raise money and awareness. We will battle alongside you with our axes left behind. To find a civil ending to what looms over these mountains and threatens our animal brothers," Hector said with sincerity and desire.

Rayne came out with tea and cornmeal biscuits. "All done." She set the tray down on the table. "Help yourselves." Sitting next to Hector, she poured herself a tea, Hayden and Hector followed suite. "What did I miss while I was gone?"

"Hayden and I have come to an understanding. He is a white man and always will be. I'm Indian and always will be." Hector softly chuckled as he drank from the cup of tea.

"Come on, Grandfather, what is that supposed to mean?"

Hector set the cup down and buttered up a biscuit. "It means, Granddaughter, that he and I have agreed that a civil ending to what looms is best. There will be no protests." Hector took a bite of the pan-fried biscuit.

Rayne smiled and nodded her head, "Well, whatever either of you said to one another, I am glad for how things turned out. When will we begin our campaign?" she questioned as she too buttered up a biscuit.

Hayden sipped from his cup of tea. "I'll get things started up once I get back home. Do you guys have access to any communications, cell phone or something?"

"Grandfather wouldn't allow any inconveniences like that," Rayne replied half-jokingly.

"I can't blame him for that. Stay in close contact with Bryce. He'll be able to relay information. It'll take at least a week, maybe two, before I'll be able to set up a few Q&A workshops. Rest assured I will be working on it. I'll get word out and get the campaign off the ground. Ultimately our goal should be to hit legislation and the public eye, before the three-week ban is lifted. Even if we don't, we'll continue the fight. The development other than minor surveying, from my understanding, can't start until six months after the government authorises the development. That decision isn't expected until September. I figure we have five months to make an impression."

"We will call the campaign, *The Coalition of Purgatory*'," Hector remarked as he nodded and smiled.

"Excellent, that's exactly what we'll call it, Hector. It's brilliant." Hayden grinned from ear to ear. Indeed the campaign needed a title, and there it was both fitting and simple. The threesome continued conversing when in the distance the harmonium of a helicopter approached. Hayden knew it was the Forestry Service and he explained to Hector and Rayne, why. "It is a shame how it ended, and I wish it could've ended differently," he added as he finished his biscuit and tea.

"Any man would have done the same if they desired to live."

"True enough, but we mustn't forget that bear probably wanted to live too." Hayden rose from the table and grabbed his pack.

Hector nodded his appreciation to Hayden's remorse, as he too stood. "You are a wise one. Sometimes to avoid death, someone or something must die. The forefathers they already forgave your actions when you saved the life of one bear to take the place of an old one. Perhaps he already suffered many defeats from old age and illness. Your bullet released him form that agony and torment. You have given him the chance to return in the hereafter, where he will be young and vibrant once again."

"Thanks. It means a lot to hear that from you," Hayden exhaled as he turned his eyes to the mountains. "Well it's getting late, almost 2:00 p.m. I have a few hour's drive still ahead. Thanks for the tea and biscuits, but I must be on my way." Hayden reached out his hand and shook Hector's then, he turned to Rayne, who was standing near, giving her a quick hug. "I'll be in touch," he assured as he stepped off the back porch.

"Be safe, Hayden, and we'll be expecting to hear from you in regard to our campaign," Rayne remarked as her and Hector waved.

"Indeed, you can count on it." Hayden waved back as he approached his truck, tossing his pack into the box. *Home sweet home, here I come,* he thought as he opened the truck door and stepped in. Looking over the dials and gages that clicked on when he turned the key, he revved the truck once, backed up, turned, and was off.

Neil, and a Forestry biologist as well as Bryce, stood next to the dead grizzly. "The rot stinks awful bad, doesn't it?" Bryce and Neil nodded, holding their breaths as best they could. "He's old no doubt about that, likely senile. I figure we harness him up, fly him out to the lab and do some tests on him," the biologist suggested. "I'd rather do that than burn the carcass. What do you think, Neil?"

"Protocol suggests we do that. I've been working these mountains for a long time, and have helped identify most of the grizzlies up here. This one, I haven't seen. We're going to have to cross-reference his DNA to see if this fellow belongs here." All in agreement they masked up and harnessed the big bear for transport. The task done, Neil and the biologist, boarded the helicopter and gave the pilot the thumbs up sign. The rotors whistled and whined as the helicopter slowly rose to the sky, the cargo dangling from its underbelly as though attached by an umbilical cord.

Bryce watched as the helicopter disappeared, taking with it the thumping echo that rattled the mountain. The scent of spring returned. No longer would he be subjected to the foul smell of the decaying carcass. He sighed as he made his way back to the tent, relieved that the threat of unwanted, hungry intruders was lessened. The reality was that intruders could appear even now.

When darkness settled that night, and flames from his fire flickered, he sat close and gazed into its flames. They soothed and reassured him, giving him both strength and mind-set. Coyotes in the distance howled. From the lake came a chorus of loons and bullfrogs. He was content. All was well at Leroy Lake. At 10:00 p.m., he hobbled to the tent and climbed into his cot.

Chapter 25

The yellow sun was making itself present when Bryce woke. A warm gentle breeze blew off the lake, and out near the middle was a cackle of Canadian geese. The honking is what drew his attention their way. He smiled as he continued his gaze. Redeemer he noticed, had already spotted the fowl, and he frolicked near the shore, not sure it would seem, if he wanted to swim out and meet them or swat at the water instead.

Bryce immediately shouldered the rifle, and with camera in hand he hobbled close to the shore, staying about twenty yards away, wanting to take a picture of Redeemer splashing at the water with the flock of geese in the background. It took a minute to set up the shot. Redeemer being the ham he was, knew exactly what was going on and showed off for the camera, making the four pictures even more creative. "Thanks, you'll be a star someday, you know that." He lowered the camera. It was true Redeemer would be a star, when the time came he'd be plastered on every wildlife magazine that Bryce could get his picture on.

The sound of sixty or more sets of wings, echoed as the cackle of geese took to flight, circled the lake, and again landed. This time further east. The cub stood on his hind legs and looked out to where they'd landed. They were small flocks on the lake now, hardly visible from where the two stood, except for their long necks. "Guess we scared them. Too bad, they were quite a sight weren't they?"

It was 9:00 a.m., when Roberto rolled out of bed. Bobbini and Nadine were busy cleaning downstairs. He sighed when he heard the vacuum. A new week for him meant phone calls, business deals, and conferences. There was also the interview he promised an Edmonton journalist; he wasn't even sure what publication it was for. After showering and shaving, Roberto dressed. Wearing jeans and a sport coat, he walked downstairs. "Good morning Bobbini, Nadine, how are you two today?" he questioned as he stopped for their reply.

"Good, very good. Today Nadine and I wash windows,

179

should only be a couple of hours. There is fresh coffee. I make it today."

"Thanks. I'll go get some right now." Roberto stepped off the last stair and entered the kitchen. Nadine followed behind with her bucket of cleaners and scrub pads.

"I'm going to scrub out the fridge and mop the kitchen floor, before heading to the outside windows," Nadine remarked as she set the bucket down.

"Sure. Have time to join me for a coffee?"

"I really shouldn't, but I will." She smirked as Roberto poured her a coffee and handed it to her.

"Thank you." Nadine brought it to her lips and gently blew. "You look nice today, Mr. Robertar. Are you going somewhere?"

"Unfortunately I am. Have a few meetings to attend in Edmonton. I will likely spend the night. You know, Nadine, today is supposed to be hot. If you like, feel free to use the pool later. I won't be around to be in your way."

"That is a nice gesture. I don't think I could take you up on it though. I'd feel like I'm intruding."

"I'm not going to be here. You wouldn't be intruding even if I were, I'm serious, Nadine, feel free. You have the front door key and know the security code to open the gate."

Nadine wanted to take him up on his offer. A swim in the pool would certainly be a great ending to a long Monday. For a minute, she contemplated. "All right, I'll take you up on your offer. You're sure it is okay?"

"Wouldn't have mentioned it if I wasn't. Feel free to use the sauna or even the hot tub. The home theatre will be free as well. Whatever you like, Nadine, feel free to use." Roberto took a drink from the coffee cup in his hand and looking at her, he smiled. How he wanted to lie in a bed with her. Nadine's own mind was racing with the same thought and desire.

Roberto was a handsome man, a real man in her mind. She had wanted to lie in a bed with him for years already. She had a crush on him that she hadn't been able to shake. It was close to a year since she'd been with a man. During that time, she resorted to other ways to satisfy her urges. The opportunity to be close to Roberto was always interrupted. Now she had the opportunity. Although he wouldn't be there, it would kind of be the same, swimming in his pool, using his sauna, hot tub, 'anything' he said. She felt tinges of desire as she continued her stare of him.

Roberto finished his coffee and looked at the time. "Well, looks like I have to head for Edmonton. Got a meeting at 1:00 p.m." Roberto set his cup in the sink, as the phone rang. Nadine who was closer, asked if she should answer it. It rang again and again, as Roberto thought about it, finally telling her to go ahead. Nadine picked up the phone and answered. "Hello, Roberto Robertar's residence."

"Hello back, who is this?"

"Nadine, Mr. Roberto's house maid."

"Hi, Nadine. This is Corbet Julliane. Is Roberto available or has he already left for Edmonton?" Nadine looked to Roberto and pointed at him, gesturing if he was available. Roberto shrugged and nodded.

"Yes, just a minute please." She pushed the hold button and handed the phone to him.

"Who is it, did they say?" he asked as he took the phone.

"Someone named Corbet."

Roberto nodded and released the hold button. "Hello Corbet how are you this morning?"

"Morning back. Glad I caught you before you headed this way. Mr. Cathwyn cancelled today's meeting, would like to reschedule for mid-week or early next week."

Roberto rubbed his chin. "How come he cancelled?"

"Didn't say."

"All right. Ah...hmm, do you have my itinerary near?" There was a pause on the other end.

"Got it now."

"Can you tell me what time my interview with that journalist is for tomorrow? At least I think it might be tomorrow, give me his name and for what publication, if it's handy."

"Yep, right here. It's with Andrew Michaels from the Eastern News. It's for tomorrow at 2:30 p.m. at the Edmonton office."

"Can you change it? Make it for Monday next week, early morning preferably. That meeting with Cathwyn, make for Monday as well, say, sometime in the afternoon."

"All right. You have a few other meetings this week, but they're not really pressing. Want those changed for next week too?"

"Yeah, that would be best. I'll do homework this week. Fax over the plans for the Purgatorys, White Swan, and that development up north, and any other crap I might need to look at. Transfer any calls to my home office. I'll be here."

"No problem. I'll phone you later with the particulars for next week."

"Yep, talk to you later." Roberto hung up the phone. Nadine was outside in the courtyard washing the French sliding glass door. He walked over and slid it opened. "That was the office in Calgary. My meeting for today was cancelled. Looks like I'm going to be here after all. I was thinking if you still want to go for a swim and take me up on my offer, I'll throw in a barbecue. Got some real nice steaks. What do you say? Just a friendly get together is all."

She almost fell over backward. The thought of dinning with Roberto was a dream come true. Perhaps all those years of longing for him would finally pay off. "Gee, I don't know what to say, Mr. Robertar," she responded, playing hard to get.

"Forget the Mr. Call me Roberto. Come on, Nadine, you and your mother have done such a great job for me over the years. Let me at least show you my gratitude by barbecuing you a steak."

She was silent as she contemplated the idea. The tinge of desire returned and she smiled. "All right, you're on." She averted her eyes to the glass door once more and continued scrubbing it, afraid to stand that he might notice her hardening nipples.

"Excellent. I'll see you tonight then?" he confirmed. Turning he made his way to his home office. Nadine was all giddy, smiling at what might take place, as butterflies danced in her stomach.

Roberto booted up his desktop computer and went over some development plans of a few different projects that Robertar & Robertar had on the back burner. One was for a hotel/casino in Alberta, another for a ranch type resort in British Columbia's Big Sheep Valley. Neither one he wanted to move on yet. They were insignificant as compared to the other developments that were in the making. Besides, his hope was that JR would join him in those two ventures. Looking them over once more he closed the files.

The company's financial records were next. He went through the ones he had access to. The others were accessed through the Edmonton office. Going through them with a fine tooth-comb, he was pleased that they were in order. A few phone calls came through, and before he knew it, it was 4:00 p.m., Nadine and Bobbini had long been gone and the house was silent.

Rising from his desk, he shut down the computer, turned off the phone and exited the office. He wasn't sure what time Nadine would arrive, neither one had said a time. He could only hope she would. She seemed a bit evasive, and Roberto hoped it wasn't because she was afraid to be alone with him. He had every intention on being a gentleman. He wasn't going to put moves on her, not this time at least. He only wanted the company, and to get to know her a bit better rather than knowing her as only one of his maids. He felt guilty in a sense, as he reminisced. He was forty-eight, twenty years older at least. *Hell she's twenty-seven, maybe even closer to twenty-eight, and old enough to make her own decisions,* he thought.

Making his way into the kitchen, he pulled the big Black Angus T-bone steaks from the freezer and tossed them on a plate. They'd defrost in about two hours and be ready for the barbecue by 7:00 p.m. If Nadine didn't show, he'd cook them both anyway. Opening the fridge he pulled out a Pepsi and cracked it open. Taking a long swallow he looked out the French glass door into the courtyard, watching a robin bob for worms. A few butterflies fluttered by and then up and over the concrete walls they disappeared.

Turning on his heel, he exited the kitchen. The courtyard always reminded him of Carla. She always grew flowers out there, and usually by now they would have started to bloom. Since her untimely death, all that grew there now was grass and two cedar trees. Entering the game room, he kicked on the stereo, poured himself a shot of Jack Daniel's to get a buzz started then headed upstairs to his room to get out of the clothes and to shower and shave.

Half an hour later, donning jeans and a T-shirt, he returned to the game room. After another shot of JD, he racked up the balls on the pool table. Bored with that after clearing the table for the third time, he set his cue stick down and walked over to the bar, pouring a glass of bourbon, he noted the time to be 6:00 p.m. "Time sure flies when you're having fun," he muttered with little amusement. With glass in hand, he walked to the kitchen and checked on the steaks. Thawed as they were, he set them in brine to marinate. Then into the fridge they went. *An hour or two and you guys will be ready for heat,* he thought as he closed the fridge door.

Fifteen minutes later, after cleaning up his mess and wiping the counters down, he saw the orange light flicker on the security monitor. Looking, he was enthralled to see Nadine drive up. He met her at the door. "Hello, I was beginning to think you stood me up."

"Would never do that, especially when steaks are involved." She was wearing a tight white jump suit and underneath that, one could see a blue thong bikini.

"Excellent, they're marinating as we speak. Come on in. Would you like a drink?"

"I'd love a glass of wine," she said, setting her night bag down.

"Your wish is my command. Follow me and you can pick out whatever one you want."

"Thanks, lead the way." The two walked into the game room and over to the wine rack. "Wow, quite the assortment. I'd love a glass of this CG Garden Gold. I have drunk it before and loved it."

Roberto handed her a wineglass. "It's one of my favourites too. It tops my list. Probably one of the best white wines I've had."

"No kidding," Nadine replied as she took a long swallow. Looking to the pool table, she smiled. "Care for a game?" Nadine Macastov unbeknownst to Roberto, was a four-time woman's billiard champion, but she wasn't about to tell him. Not yet at least.

"You play?" Roberto asked.

"A little bit." Nadine walked over to the rack of pool cues on the wall and admired them.

"Sure then. I'll rack them up." Roberto made his way to the pool table. "There are some really great cues in that collection. Feel free to use whatever one you like. If you can't find one in that rack that you like, open the doors to your left and there are some more." Roberto finished racking up the balls.

Nadine had already made her selection; it was the Tempest 16.oz. The shaft was a specially selected grade of hard rock Canadian maple, and was fitted with a Le Pro tip. "I love the look of this one. It's a lucky cue I think." Nadine approached the table.

"That is a great cue, but luck has nothing to do with billiards." Roberto smiled. "Ladies first," he said as he gestured for Nadine to break the balls.

"Actually, Mr. Robertar," Nadine started before Roberto interjected.

"Please, call me Roberto."

"Sorry, Roberto. I think you should go first. I haven't played in quite some time." she fibbed.

"Okay." Roberto lined up the cue ball to the right of the triangle of balls at the end of the table, slamming the cue ball it smashed into them, scattering the set and sinking four, two high's and two lows. Roberto looked at his shot. "I'll call high ball," he said as he lined up another shot. Missing the hit, he shook his head. "That was bad. Your turn."

Nadine stepped up to the table, lined up her shot and

made it without a hitch.

"That was a pretty good shot, wow," Roberto commented from the side.

"Luck I think," she responded as she set up for her second shot. Roberto never got a second chance to try and sink anymore of his balls. Nadine cleared the table, "I knew this cue was lucky," she said as she turned and looked at Roberto. Who stood dumbfounded and shocked. "Best two out of three?" Nadine smirked as she took a drink from her wineglass.

"Most definitely. I haven't been beaten that quickly before," Roberto said with humor, as he set up the balls once more and Nadine broke them. They played another game and Roberto came out on top. The third and final game of course, went Nadine's way as she cleared the table in less time than the first time. "I have an inclination to think you've played a lot?" Roberto commented as he smiled. "If you haven't, you're damn lucky."

Nadine was sitting on one of the leather chairs, sipping wine and smiling. She still wasn't going to tell him that she was a pro. "Maybe we should play again after a swim in the pool?" she hinted.

"Definitely. Like I said, I've never been beaten that quickly, and especially not twice." Roberto poured himself some bourbon. "Care for a glass of Wild Turkey?"

"No thanks, maybe later. For now I'll stick to the wine." She rose from the chair and poured another glass. "Are we going swimming now?"

"By all means." They walked the short distance to the outdoor pool. Nadine slipped out of the white jump suit she was wearing, to reveal a killer blue thong bikini. Roberto swallowed deep. She was magnificent. It was hard for him to stop staring. She noticed, smiling to herself as she dove in. Roberto watched as she swam the distance of the pool and back again.

"Aren't you going to join me?" The truth was Roberto never learned to swim, the pool was for Carla while she was alive, and JR as he grew. Roberto had never swum in it.

Nadine could tell by the look in his eye that he was fishing for an excuse. "You don't know how to swim, do you?"

Roberto felt like an idiot. "No actually I don't." he said straightforward, and somewhat embarrassed.

"I won't let you drown. Come on. The water is beautiful," she coaxed. He wanted nothing more than to join her, except he couldn't find the courage.

"Go ahead. I really have an issue with water," he half joked, shrugging his shoulders.

Nadine continued gazing at him, and smiled. *He's such a sweet guy,* she thought. She didn't want to put him on the spot. "All right," she relented, swimming to the diving board. He watched her as she bounced once then twice then finally dove. She swam the distance of the sixty-foot pool a couple more times then stepped out. Roberto handed her a towel.

"That was some great diving you did. Are you good at everything, or what?"

"Only the things I like," she said as she sat down on a poolside lounge chair next to him. The scent of her body as it wafted toward him, was that of strawberries. He inhaled deeply.

"I hope you don't think I'm an ass, but, you smell terrific."

"Why would I think you are an ass for that?"

Roberto shrugged. "I don't know. I didn't want it to sound like I was coming on to you. You truly smell terrific."

Nadine was smiling as she looked at him. She wanted to put moves on him, but not yet. Now wasn't the time. "It's my shampoo, Strawberry Ice it's called."

Roberto looked at her and nodded. "It smells nice," he responded, as he looked her over as inconspicuously as he could. "Want to check out the sauna?" he suggested.

"That would be great. I'd love to."

"Great, I'll go turn it on." He stood and walked back into the house. She watched him as he slipped out of sight. She was longing for his touch, for his hands to caress her. Taking another quick swim, Roberto returned as she finished the lap. "Sauna is ready and waiting," he commented as he waited for her. She stepped out of the pool and grabbed the towel, bottle of wine and her glass.

"Can we drink in there?" she coyly asked as she strutted passed him.

"I do." He followed behind. Opening the door, the two stepped in.

"Oh, this is beautiful," she said as she made her way to a bench and sat down. The four speakers in each of the corners played soft music. Closing her eyes, she swayed her head back and forth to the sound, a big smile across her face. "You like classical music?"

"Sure do. I can change it if you like."

"No. I love it. It's quite fitting music to take a sauna with." She poured another glass of wine and brought the glass to her cherry mouth. Roberto watched as she took a swallow. She smiled at him. "What, what did I do?" she teased.

"I'm sorry I didn't mean to be staring."

"Quit apologising. I don't mind. I like it when you stare at me," Nadine revealed, starting to feel a buzz from the wine.

Roberto raised an eyebrow and he smiled back. "I can't help it, you're a beautiful woman. A fellow like me doesn't have the opportunity every day to look at such beauty." He too was beginning to feel a buzz from the bourbon. Indeed, she was eye candy.

"Maybe you'd like to see more of me?" she teased, as she stood and sat on his lap.

Roberto was shocked as she pushed his head into her bosom and began kissing his neck. He didn't stop her.

Finally she rolled onto her side, running a finger down his chest. "Shall we shower and play some more pool?" she teased.

Chapter 26

At 5:30 a.m., Roberto rolled over to see that Nadine still lie at his side. *What is Bobbini going to say when she sees her daughter coming out of my room,* he thought as he continued his gaze upon her. He shook her, "Nadine, Nadine, wake up. What's your mother going to say? She should be her in the next while," he said with both dread and concern. Bobbini would have him by the nuts if she found out, especially this way.

Nadine opened her eyes and smiled. "I told her last night that I would do your place alone today, and do it I shall." She chuckled in her tired state. "Mother needed a rest. It didn't take much to convince her." She closed her eyes again and drifted back to sleep. Roberto sat there, his mind dancing with the past evening activities, relieved Nadine had already taken care of a possible encounter with her mother.

"Thank God," he muttered, as he too lay back down. At 9:00 a.m., the phone rang, Roberto reached over and picked it up. "Good morning."

"Good morning, Roberto, this is Foster."

"How are you?"

"Not bad. You wanted me to call you in regard to getting a possible subcontractor up in the Purgatorys. Plus I have the name of that BC backbencher who got the land development ban set in stone."

"Who would that be?"

"A fellow named Conrad Jackson, he's also the big boss at the Kootenay Forestry Service. I think you know him."

There was a pause at Roberto's end. "Yep, I know him. He's also the guy who hired that Bryce fellow who is up at Leroy Lake snooping around."

"Yes, that's him, the one and only, Conrad Jackson."

"Not much we can do in that regard. I'm glad you came up with the name though. Anyway, as for a subcontractor going up there, I think we should hire a private citizen. The ban states that we can't hire any subcontractors, says nothing about a plain Joe."

Foster chuckled, "Yeah, I read through the papers too. Have anyone in mind?"

"Nope. I'll leave that up to the Edmonton office. I'll fill them in though. Unless you'd like to do that?"

"All right I'll get on it. Do we want a surveyor or a photographer or both?"

"No need for photos, not yet at least. A surveyor though would certainly put us ahead of the game. Even if we get him or her up there at the end of the week. That'd give a surveyor a two-week run. We want someone good not a novice. Can you manage that Foster?"

"Sure can, have a short list already compiled."

"Excellent. That's why I keep you guys around." Roberto chuckled. "Anything else? I take it we have Strangehaur & Field still in our pocket?"

"Yeah, for now. Not sure, how long they'll want to ride with us though. They were pretty vague when I spoke to them yesterday."

"Ah, they decide to run with their tails between their legs, just let them go. I know twenty-three million is a nice investment, I think if need be, Robertar & Robertar could dig deep enough and cover their kitty."

"There's no doubt about that. It'll hurt for a while though."

"We've been hurt before." Roberto grew silent.

"I suppose. All right, I got some work to do. I'll get back to you once I decide whom to send up to the Purgatorys."

"Make sure you tell whoever you decide, to keep clear of Leroy Lake. We don't need that Bryce fellow catching wind of them being up there. Otherwise, we'll likely be looking at that ten-million-dollar fine."

"Don't need that kind of press."

"No kidding."

"Okay, I'll make sure they stay clear of the lake."

"Right on. Get back to me once you send someone up there."

"Count on it, Roberto, talk to you then. Bye for now." Foster hung up the phone.

Roberto looked over to Nadine and smiled. *Guess I'll let her sleep,* he thought as he rose. A hot shower and coffee, were on top of his morning list.

On a hunch, Bryce booted up his laptop. He was hoping to have received an email from Hayden. It had only been two days since he'd left, and chances were he hadn't been able to get too far along with their campaign. Bryce was surprised when indeed there was an email waiting for him and that it was from Hayden. "Cool," he muttered as he clicked it on and opened it.

The email explained that Hector and Rayne agreed to deal with the Purgatory development in a civil way, and that they wouldn't proceed with the protests. That the campaign was now registered as 'The Coalition of Purgatory' and that he managed all the legalities of a fundraiser. Donation boxes were going to be put out by mid-week. He added in the email that he donated a lump sum of four million at Colleen's request.

She had taken it upon herself to do most of the footwork, and was currently doing her best in researching and contacting the Conservatory for Environment cause. "Excellent," Bryce said out loud, as he continued to read it. It was signed by 'the happy fisherman.' Chuckling, he shut the laptop down. Rising from the chair, he exited into the morning light. He was seated at the table outside for only a short while when he heard the clip-clop of a horse, looking in the direction of the sound, he was ecstatic to see Rayne approach. "Rayne," he said with a smile as he stood and greeted her. "Wasn't expecting anyone. Glad to see you."

"Morning. How is it going?" she asked as she dismounted.

"Pretty good. I have coffee on, can I interest you in a cup."

"Of course," Rayne responded as they walked. "Where is that cub of yours?"

Bryce shrugged. "I've been letting him go about his own business. He'll show up sooner or later." He poured them each a coffee and he handed one to Rayne.

"Thanks." She sat next to him. "It's a gorgeous day today isn't it?"

"Yeah, yesterday was decent too. How have you and Hector been?" He took a drink from his cup.

"Good. I would've showed up earlier except Grandfather hasn't been feeling well lately. Today he finally told me to take a ride, that I needed some fresh air. I think he knew I was coming here 'cause he said he'd see me in the morning." She was smiling.

"You mean you're going to spend the night?" he asked with hope and desire.

"Yep. All day too."

"Wow, that's great. I'm happy about that."

"About what? That I'm here, or that you get to have me any way you want?" she joked and baited.

"About all of it." He was smiling; he felt like a teenager at the prom, and his queen was Rayne. "Later do you want to take stroll along the lake? Might get a chance to see some geese. They've been hanging out here for a day or two. A cackle of sixty or so?"

"Certainly." She brought the cup of coffee to her lips and took a swallow. "Have you seen any more bears? They should be showing themselves soon."

"Yeah, actually Hayden spotted a black bear and two cubs a few days ago. Did he tell you about the grizzly he put to rest?"

"He did. Lucky for him he had the rifle. I always worry about that happening to you."

"I suppose it could. I'm cautious though. Especially now with this cast on. Besides the bears and I understand one another." Bryce chuckled.

"When do you get the cast off?"

"A couple more weeks. I wish I could take it off now, cause it's awful itchy and driving me batty."

"I bet. I had a broken arm once. Drove me batty." Rayne looked toward the lake spotting a deer and fawn. "Look." she whispered as she pointed.

Bryce turned his head and smiled. "Isn't that

something." Just then Redeemer darted out of the undergrowth, startling the deer and her fawn. They hightailed it into the forest. "Redeemer you spoiled our view," Bryce commented, as the cub dashed to Rayne's side and sniffed her. Then he rolled over exposing his belly, expecting her to rub it.

"Isn't that sweet," she responded, giving him a good belly rub. "You're sure growing." She was laughing as she continued rubbing his belly. "What a little cutie pie. Stinky, but cute," she added. Redeemer looked at her with his big brown eyes then rolled back onto all four's and walked toward her horse. Bryce and Rayne watched as the fun and games began.

Redeemer would dart toward the horse, stop, and rise on his hind legs. The horse would snort, lower its head and shake it from side to side. Redeemer followed suit, doing the same thing back. Finally the horse moved toward him and the cub dropped to all four's, running behind the tent. Rayne and Bryce watched with amusement and laughed. "Isn't that something, they remember that game from before."

"Yeah, no kidding," Bryce commented. "Wonder if Gravy Train thinks it's a game?"

"For sure he does. Isn't that right, Gravy Train," Rayne said to her horse as she stood and walked over to him, removing his saddle and reins. "There that'll give you some more freedom. Don't be going too far, stay close," she said as she turned and carried the items back to the tent, setting them down under the awning.

"You don't have to tether him?"

"Nope, he'll stay close. Always has. What do you want to do, Bryce? I feel like a walk. Maybe we could take that stroll along the lake now?"

"By all means. Sure thing." Bryce rose from the table. "Do you want to pack the rifle or the camera?" he teased knowing he could handle both.

"The camera."

He handed her the camera, giving her a quick rundown on how it worked. They coursed their way to the distance rock bluffs on the north-east shore, talking between themselves as they did. "It was around here somewhere that Hayden saw the bear and her cubs." Bryce looked out across the lake. "Look there are the geese," he said as he pointed to them.

"Aren't they beautiful? Can I snap a few pictures?"

"Of course, please do." He watched as Rayne went to work. She handled the camera like a pro. The camera clicked and buzzed as she snapped five or six pictures.

"There, I think I got some good pictures." Rayne walked back to where Bryce stood. "You look a bit tired. Maybe we should sit for a bit."

"Not so tired, but am sure feeling the leg. Yeah, sitting is a good idea." He handed Rayne the rifle so she could set it down. Then she helped him to the ground, sitting next to him on the grassy shore.

"What a great view," Rayne commented as she looked out across the lake. The warm gentle breeze tousled their hair, blowing it this way and that. Sitting in silence they took in the view, soaking up the rays from the early morning sun. Life was good.

Lying down, Bryce put his hands behind his head and looked up to the heavens. Not a cloud was in the sky. It was clear, blue, and majestic. The sun beat down on him and he closed his eyes. Rayne's soft lips caressed his cheek and he opened one eye. She was looking at him with a smile across her face. "You looked so peaceful that I had to kiss you."

"Kiss away," he urged, as she lay next to him. It was difficult making love on the hard ground with his leg in a cast, but they managed. They frolicked a while longer, laughing, and giggling, like two high school kids. Satisfied, they lay motionless staring to the heavens. Rayne finally sat up and dressed then helped Bryce pull his pants up and helped him to his feet.

"For an invalid you sure know how to perform," she teased as he dusted himself off.

He chuckled. "If there is one thing a man will always be able to do, no matter what his state, that would be it."

"How many times do you suppose we could do it before morning?" Rayne teased with a smile, as she turned and dared him.

He felt his cheeks go flush, *how am I going to answer that,* he thought, smiling wryly. "Yikes, that's a question I'd never thought I'd need to answer."

Rayne started to snicker, bringing the camera up to her eye, snapping a few pictures of the look on his face as he tried to answer. Then she turned and playfully ran ahead. Bryce shook his head as he hobbled after her. Finally, making the distance back to the tent they sat, out of breath and laughing as though they were both mad. Least that's how it looked from Redeemer's point of view, as he sat idly by and watched. They fooled around and joked a while longer, eventually turning their attention to the campaign and discussed it further.

Rayne wanted to know if Hayden had yet emailed him. Bryce told her that he had, and what he'd been able to accomplish so far. She was shocked at the donation Hayden had contributed, and asked a few questions. None of which, Bryce could answer, for Hayden's obscurity and his own promise that he made. He felt stupid for saying it came from Hayden. Covering his tracks, he made it sound as though Hayden raised the money privately through a few investors he knew.

"That's a lot of money for one guy to raise, but what a contribution. That's amazing; he must know some heavy investors."

"That's what I said." Bryce shrugged his shoulders. "Want more coffee?" he asked, trying to change the subject, or at least the subject in regard to Hayden and his donated funds.

Rayne nodded. "Sure, I'd love another cup. What else did Hayden have to say? He mentioned he was going to set up a Q&A for Grandfather and me to try and raise some funds as well?"

"He mentioned that as well; said it was coming along fine. Said he'd know more in a week or two." He turned on the camp stove, adding water and some fresh grounds to the coffee-pot. "Oh yeah, donation boxes are being put out some time this week as well, locally I presume in grocery stores, banks and such."

"Wow. He sure moves fast doesn't he?"

"Actually, I think it is his wife, Colleen who jump-starts everything." Bryce chuckled.

"True enough, she's a go-getter. I met her a couple of times."

"Isn't that weird that we've both known Hayden and Colleen, yet, not until I met you here did I know Hector had such a beautiful Granddaughter. Weird I'd say." He set the pot on the glowing flame.

"Grandfather and Hayden, met back in 1997 or 1998. Grandfather used his outfit to track a wounded grizzly bear near Toby Creek. Hayden has always teased Grandfather about that."

"I remember Hayden mentioning that a long time ago. Wasn't Hector hurt?"

"That's why he contacted Hayden. The bear attacked Grandfather, dislocated his hip, and broke his collarbone. He also scratched him up. That was why Grandfather shot him. He made his way back to his cabin, saddled up Gravy Train, and headed to the lower road. He was found in the ditch passed out from shock, with Gravy Train at his side. When he came to in the hospital a day or two later, he contacted the nearest outfitter, which happened to be Hayden's. They've been friends since," Rayne explained as she reminisced.

"Hence the walking stick," Bryce said.

"Yep, he carved it after he healed and was well enough to do so. It took him forever. Three times that I visited him after that, he was still carving it. The finished product though, was and is magnificent, isn't it?"

"Sure is. I've never seen a carving quite like that, ever." The coffee now done, he poured each of them a cup. "Here's to Hector and his awesome carving," Bryce joked as he rose his coffee cup and took a drink. Hours burned away as they reminisced, talking about this, that, and nothing at all. Before they realised it, dusk approached. The western sky was an added bonus to an excellent day, with colours of red, pink and mauve, behind that the sun's rays reflected a pallid yellow. Both he and Rayne looked on in awe. "Shall we walk over to the fire pit? A fire tonight would be great."

"Can we bring blankets?"

"For a night like this and an earlier dare, you bet. I'll get the fire going if you get the blankets."

"You're on. Meet you there," Rayne teased as she turned and entered the tent to fetch the blankets. Shouldering the rifle, he hobbled over to the fire pit. Getting the flames going took a minute, but he managed. By the time Rayne showed, the flames were snapping, crackling, and dancing on the breeze. She laid out the blanket and sat next to him. "I can't get over that sunset. My God, it looks as though it was painted by Michelangelo. Isn't it awesome? Should I go and get your camera?"

There was no denying it the sunset was spectacular and he nodded, "Excellent idea. If it's not a problem, that would be great. A few pictures of that would only add to the repertoire. You can even take them. How does that sound? You seem to have knack with the lens."

"Thanks." She rose and made her way back to the tent to retrieve the camera. "Do you have more film?" she called out from the tent.

"Yep, it's in the camera case. Feel free to grab one."

"Will do," she responded as she shuffled through the case, finding a new roll she turned and made her way back to the fire and Bryce's side. "Got one. There's two more frames left on the old one. Smile pretty," she said, snapping the last two frames. "There all gone." She smiled. "Now, how do I go about reloading film?" She handed it to Bryce and shrugged.

Smiling he explained to her how to load and reload film, showing her the buttons to press to activate each process. "Basically it's all automatic except of course removing the film from the camera," he chuckled.

"Neat, it's not much different than mine. Except mine is completely done manually and most times is a real pain."

"True enough, I've used them old fellows. In fact, some of the photos in my earlier articles were all done with an old Pentax, K1000.35mm. I was lucky and had two lenses, a Takumar telephoto lens, as well as a lens that came with the outfit. Takes excellent pictures. This one is a Pentax 35mm as well. They say this model is the heart of the Pentax line."

"Mine is a Nikon, something, something. I have two lenses as well. Not sure the brand or type." Rayne smirked as she took the camera from him. "I haven't used mine much." She brought the camera to her eye and focused on Bryce. "Tell me, if that's how you describe a camera, how would you describe me?" She chuckled as he looked at her.

"I'd describe you as a Rayne Bow of colour. The most beautiful one I've ever seen." He was showing his pearly whites and she snapped a couple of frames. Bryce shook his head, "Go on, take some pictures of that sunset," he joked, as he tried grabbing the camera from her.

"In due time. Now raise that leg of yours with that dirty white cast. I want a picture of that." Bryce raised his leg and made a funny face. "You're a ham, you and Redeemer make a good pair." Rayne snapped a couple more frames of Bryce's antics. Lowering the camera, she smiled. "All right, next on the list is that sunset, smile pretty sunset," she instructed as she focused on it. Taking her time, she made the pictures as creative as she could, snapping six frames. Satisfied, she sat next to Bryce. "Did as best I could, Mr. Bryce," she joked, "I hope they turn out," she added with a more serious note.

"I'm sure they will," Bryce assured her as she curled up to him. "Beautiful night isn't it?" he softly spoke as he wrapped his arm around her shoulder.

"Yes it is. It's even more beautiful with you in it."

He chuckled, "Right back at you. Right back at you." He squeezed her shoulder. *Everything is beautiful when a Rayne Bow is in it,* he thought as he kissed the top of her head, staring into the flames. The fire that evening was obviously not the only flame burning. After making love for the second time that day, spent and tired they rose and retreated to the tent. They made a bed for two on the floor. Once his leg was comfortable, in unison, they fell into a slumber of contentment.

Chapter 27

Rayne left for Toby Creek the following day at 10:00 a.m., leaving Bryce with a smile across his face. Their meetings at Leroy Lake blossomed as days and weeks came and went, *true love it was.* The cub grew to become independent, and by July was rarely seen. It was sad in a sense, yet Bryce knew it was Redeemer's calling to return to the Purgatorys. On occasion, when he did spot Redeemer while he continued with his work, it was always from a distance. *Man and beast, had grown apart.* It was as Hector had said, Bryce had given the bear a new lease on life, and for that reason Bryce found it comforting that Redeemer chose his own destiny, and that the Purgatorys would be his home.

Days turned to weeks, and weeks into months. Roberto Robertar filed a lawsuit in the Supreme Court of Canada in early August, citing interference from the Coalition, the Legislation, as well as the Conservation Forestry Service, arguing that it was illegal and that it should be rejected as untrue, unfounded, or unjust. The Coalition of Purgatory was now a thorn in his side. By the end of August, the Coalition had a surplus of seven million dollars and donations kept coming.

Fundraisers, workshops, and debates at local schools and colleges were set up weekly, featuring Hector and Rayne as speakers for the Coalition. Surprise guests and VIP's, were featured as time allowed. It was a campaign of awareness, reason, and fact. Posters popped up and articles on the development began to surface in magazines, newspapers. TV, radio broadcasts, and interviews with those who opposed it, and those who didn't, were seen and heard. Roberto's lawsuit continued.

Their battle to halt Robertar & Robertar was not futile. Only weeks before the development plans for the Purgatorys was expected to be passed, along with the helping hands of the Conservatory for Environment, they raised another five-million-dollars for a grand total of twelve-million-dollars at their disposal. With the funds backing them, the Coalition moved fast, scooping up one-third of the Purgatory range, which included Leroy Lake, abolishing any further plans or attempts by Robertar & Robertar to develop the land fully.

For Robertar & Robertar, two-thirds was better than-none, and Roberto Robertar scaled down his development plans. He continued deliberation with the Supreme Court of Canada, arguing that those involved were responsible for his company having to resort to major cutbacks, as well as the looming possibility that his company, Robertar & Robertar was faced with a pending bankruptcy. For Roberto no end was in sight, he wanted retribution for having to lay off half of his men.

The data, research, and photographic journalism, was supplied to the court by Bryce Ellwood. As well, the influence of The Coalition of Purgatory, and the Conservation/Forestry Service of New Kootenay headed by Conrad Jackson, played a big part in the outcome. The Supreme Court finally ruled that one-third of the Purgatory range held by the Conservatory for Environment, would remain unscathed, untouched, and undeveloped. Bryce's work once more made a difference. He was relieved, yet saddened that he couldn't have done more.

September 4, 2004, Bryce folded up the big canvass tent, took down the shower and porta-potty, coiled up his cables and disassembled the satellite and solar panel. It was a day of emotional distraught, a day he knew would one-day come. He and Rayne said their goodbyes two nights earlier, as the University was again in session. Now, as he sat there waiting for his helicopter flight home, he reminisced about the time he spent at Leroy Lake. Memories crossed his mind, and he rose. Picking up the old sweater he'd given to Redeemer, he folded it one last time then set it back down as a memento to the cub he grew to love, and the bear he'd never know. "Be free, Redeemer, take care and stay out of harm's way," he softly spoke as he glanced around, hoping and praying for one final look at the cub.

A tear welled up in his eye when his prayers were answered. Looking at him from a distance and hidden somewhat by the shadows, Redeemer rose on his hind legs, cocking his head as their eyes locked. Inhaling deeply Bryce's scent, as it wafted in the gentle breeze, Redeemer pawed at the air as though he were waving. A smile of contentment crossed Bryce's face, as he waved back, wiping away the single tear.

With his hand still risen, he spoke four words, "Brothers we'll always be." The distant sound of a helicopter drowned out their moment of silence, and he knew he'd never lay eyes upon the cub again. Photos and memories were all he would have. Redeemer looked back one last time then turned into the forest, and a life of his own.

Other Books by Brian T. Seifrit

Second Editions
The following books are in the process of being published in their second edition.

Red Rock Canyon
Tyrell Sloan is the heir to his Grandfather's estate, which consists of an old ramshackle cabin, and over three hundred and twenty acres of red shale, pasture, and forest. During the journey to Red Rock Canyon, he encounters a slew of unforgettable characters. He hears some unusual tales about his Grandfather and wrestles with the day-to-day survival of solitude, as he tries to make a life for himself. He learns that three of the richest gold claims in the Columbia Kootenay are on Sloan land, but all that gold, he realizes, is not worth the burden.

Escape
For Hayden Rochsoff and his two associates, brother and sister team Alex and Monique Farell, both members of the Russian Rebel Army, freedom is a dream come true... For too long their own country had held them captive.

After a futile attempt to escape from Russia, Hayden is taken into custody and tortured. He vows revenge. Joining up with the ranks of his friends, Hayden takes up a role as a sharp-shooter and becomes one of the RRA's best marksmen. He helps rescue Monique, who was captured when the RRA infiltrated a secret government agency.

Forced to kill in order to liberate his captured friends, Hayden and his associates are forced into a plan to heist sixty four million dollars from the D.E.A and U.S. Navy. The threesome are relentlessly pursued by those who wish to see them dead. Escape is their only hope.

Hayden Rochsoff finally finds safety in Canada, but his past haunts him, and he finds himself forced to take up arms again, this time to save the one he loves from life in the Russian sex trade. He uses all that he was taught in the RRA to handle the situation before the twenty-one million dollar ransom is due, by putting a bullet between the eyes of the ones who detain her.

Bloodlines

Inheriting a cattle ranch called the Double-U from a great Uncle in 1825, the Vanfells begin a treacherous journey across the Rocky Mountains. Plagued with tempestuous weather and illness, they make temporary shelters and hope that the weather and their luck will change, but they are held hostage by the elements.

An ancient, bloodthirsty curse, lying dormant, waits to strike from a hundred year slumber, and it-craves human flesh. Will the Vanfell lineage diminish to none? Will the bloodlines continue? Only Wakashan incantations and ceremonial prayers can vanquish the demonic spirit, if they're not too late.

First Editions

The following books are first editions scheduled to be released in 2014.

Return to Red Rock

Six years after leaving behind his inheritance, Tyrell Sloan returns to familiar ground. In 1890, he was the heir to the estate of his Grandfather, John Henry Sloan Sr. consisting of 300 acres of red shale, forest, and pasture. Near the homestead, and less than an hour's ride up stream of the Hudu Creek, were three gold claims, the Sloan 1, 2 and 3. At the time of his departure, the claims were contracted for a two-year term with the Wake Up Jake, a mining company.

When he left, he wrote a letter that he stashed in the sacks of gold put in Grandma Heddy's care. Tyrell bequeathed the gold to Grandma, and his share of whatever the Wake Up Jake produced during the term of the contract. To Marissa, he left the homestead, all 300 acres.

With plans to head north to his hometown of Hell's Bottom, he was side tracked. A recurring dream of his Grandfather's death and the men who killed him, as well as the face-to-face encounter with the villainous men of his dream, took over the next six years of his life.

With the possibility of being captured and hanged, Tyrell returns to Red Rock Canyon to live his life in obscurity. To his surprise, Marissa, his onetime true love continues to reside there. It isn't long before the two are once more reacquainted, and their adventure begins as Tyrell tries to right his wrongs from days gone past.

Voracity

Voracity follows a team of researchers and field assassins that work for the elite K.A.T. (Kuru Assault Team) Agency, as they search for a cure for a disease derived from the Kuru virus. A young neurologist, Trent Sweet discovered it. Papers he wrote and submitted to medical magazines and health organisations were dismissed as fiction. Trent died a gruesome death for the cause in 1994. The circumstances would always haunt his brother Blain.

The Agency has a purpose that Blain endorses so he continues on, building up the Agency to what it is today. So secret is the K.A.T Agency that few in the Canadian Government or law enforcement agencies know of its existence.

Blain is the Agency's finest and most elite assassin. He is assigned to do some field research, a part of his job that he detests. During this research, he discovers there is more to K-15 then anyone had expected.

Other Books

Chased by Shadows

This is a remarkably candid and riveting read about the life and struggles of a young boy as he grows into manhood. It's not the usual "coming of age story." In Chased By Shadows, you will learn the loves and hates of a soul destined to walk the hot coals of life as he struggles to find his true identity, his true path, and eventually, his true love.

This story has been required reading two years running for the "Justice Studies" course at St. Lawrence College in Kingston, Ontario.

Absolute Anger

"Absolute Anger" is a story of intrigue and suspense revolving around Detective Tyler O'Brien, promoted to lieutenant since he and his crew of brash detectives captured the man responsible for four brutal and deranged killings. The trial and sentencing of the murderer should have ended the crime spree, but that was just the beginning...

O'Brien learns that the killer has escaped from prison. Following a trail of corpses from the streets of Toronto, the evidence leads him and his crew into the barren mountain passes of British Columbia, and finally back to the location of the killer's earliest crimes in an increasingly dangerous manhunt for a deranged and psychotic killer. As fate would have it only death can be the outcome.

This "edge of the seat" thriller has been optioned by Mad Samurai Films Inc., in Toronto.

A Bloodstained Hammer (with Alison Townsend MacNicol)

This is the story of a hog-farming family, the Townsends, living in the Kootenays in British Columbia, Canada in the late 1950's and later years. The story describes the hard life for the farmer who has to work at a nearby mine and smelter in order to support his farm work. The story is a fictionalized description based on the actual events that occurred. Of course, the conversations, thoughts expressed and activities are the product of the authors' imaginations. The fact that the events are still so clearly remembered fifty years later is significant, indicating the depth to which the events affected the family.

Family day-to-day life is described. The need for hired help is satisfied when a young man answers their advertisement. He joins the family, works hard, learns the ropes of hog farming and butchering. The hired man, called Hudulak in the story, has a number of problems related to his limited intelligence, his sexual desires and his drinking to excess on the few occasions he goes out on the town. These problems are not noted especially by the Townsend family, although the eight year old daughter Emily is unhappy with the way he leers at her.

Hudulak goes on a drinking binge with a neighbor and ends up in Mrs. Townsend's bedroom in the middle of the night. Mr. Townsend is working the night shift. Unfortunately, the confrontation in the bedroom leads to the death of both Mrs. Townsend and Emily, the eight year old. Hudulak cleans up a little and drives away in the family car.

Although he is caught within a few hours, he is able to convince the authorities that he is insane and his only punishment is a life of leisure in a mental hospital for 18 years. Eventually, he is given a complete release, marries and lives a normal life.

In the meantime, life goes on for the remnants of the Townsend family. The effect of this crime on the family is described, and the frustration felt by the family members by the ineffective way in which the crimes were handled is lamented. The Townsends believe that the Canadian Justice system failed and believe that Hudulak simply fooled all the authorities.

Based on a true story, the authors get inside the minds of the characters, describing the thoughts and feelings of a murderer and his victims.

A free workbook for the use of ESL students and teachers to aid in studying the text is available on the Publisher's website. The student will have the opportunity to correct the grammar.

Due to the descriptions of the sexually explicit thoughts of the hired hand, the story is unsuitable for public school children.

Although the insanity defence is still in vogue today, the Townsends believe that today's psychiatrists and prosecutors would not be quite so lenient as they were in the 1960's in a remote area in the interior of B.C. Interestingly, in 2012, a mental patient in Quebec who killed his children and was found not guilty by reason of insanity was given a full discharge after only two years of treatment. This story shows the impact these crimes have on the victims.

Biography of Brian T. Seifrit

Brian is a seven-time published author. In September 1988-December-1989, he attended Columbia Academy of Radio, Television & Recording Arts, in Calgary, AB, where he majored in Broadcast Journalism. Following that, and ten years later, he attended Selkirk College in Castlegar BC, from September 1999-April 2001 where he was Enrolled in UT Courses – English History, Philosophy, Creative Writing, and Canadian Literature and majored in Print Journalism.

He has been happily married for 27 years and counting. He has four children, two from previous relationships, and two with his current wife. He grew up on a small hobby farm outside of Fruitvale BC.

In 2000, he wrote for the Source a community newspaper in Fruitvale BC, and since then has done freelance writing of human interest for the Trail Daily Times.

When he writes for himself, he tries not to stay in only one genre, He finds that one genre gets stale after a while. Instead he chooses to write in as many genres as he can. Imagination and creativity are wonderful tools, and he uses them both. From the list of the titles and brief descriptions above, you will undoubtedly agree that Brian is a multi-faceted writer with a vivid imagination.

Any communications with Brian can be emailed to:

tbseifrit@gmail.com

Your ESL Story Publishers Ltd.

This publishing house was established in September 2012 for the purpose of self-publishing the stories by William Jenkins. These stories are intended to be supplementary reading for elementary school students (about Grade 5) learning English as a Second Language, hence the ESL in the company name.

Brian and William have yet to meet, although they did communicate years ago when Brian was writing his first book, "Chased by Shadows".

When Brian's previous publisher decided not to handle new books, Brian and William got together to keep some of Brian's books available.

Any communications with the publisher can be emailed to:

Bill@yourstorypublishers.ca.

Information on how to order these books is available at website:

https://yourstorypublishers.ca

31134686R00123

Made in the USA
Charleston, SC
07 July 2014